THE UNSELFISHNESS OF GOD

The Unselfishness Of God

Hannah Whitall Smith

LITTLEBROOK PUBLISHING, INC. PRINCETON, NEW JERSEY 08540

THE UNSELFISHNESS OF GOD
   by Hannah Whitall Smith

This edited edition
© 1987 Littlebrook Publishing, Inc., Princeton, NJ 08540.
All rights reserved.
Printed in the United States of America.

Special thanks for jacket photo and drawing of Mrs. Smith to
Barbara Strachey, who included them in her book, *Remarkable
Relations: The Story of the Pearsall Smith Women* (Universe
Books, New York).

Library of Congress Cataloging-in-Publication Data

Smith, Hannah Whitall, 1832-1911.
   The Unselfishness of God.

   1. Smith, Hannah Whitall, 1832-1911. 2. Christian biography.
3. Holiness. I. Title.
BR1725.S53A3   1987   289.6'3 [B]   87-26290
ISBN 0-89952-087-1

CONTENTS

FOREWORD

Everything I knew about Hannah Whitall Smith had come from her classic, *A Christian's Secret of a Happy Life*. Then, a friend suggested if I wanted to really understand this fascinating Christian I should try to locate her spiritual autobiography, a turn-of-the-century volume long out of print.

When I finally found a tattered copy of *The Unselfishness of God* I read it with total absorption. Hannah Whitall Smith was even more amazing than I had suspected. Blessed with both a first class mind and a talent for expressing it, she was relentless, indefatigable, in her search for spiritual truth. Not only did she want to understand every aspect of God's character and nature, she wanted to know specifically what He expected of her.

For a long time her inquiry begged an answer. As a teenager growing up in a well-to-do family of Philadelphia Quakers, she says that she believed God *would* save her, but "only if she could somehow make herself worthy of being saved." Thus feeling caught between a rock and a hard place, young Hannah struggled to understand God's grace, but like her biblical namesake her trust was not in vain.

What great encouragement her story of groping and uncertainty is for all of us who daily fall short of His high calling. And what great drama to read how this one of little faith grew in unity and harmony with God until she was a teacher and preacher of His truths to millions.

"All of our dealings with God are for the purpose of bringing us into oneness with Himself," she stated in *The Christian's Secret of a Happy Life*. "All steps in the Christian life lead up to this. The Lord has made us for it; and until we have intelligently apprehended it, and have voluntarily consented to embrace it, our hearts have not found their destined and real rest."

Mrs. Smith knew whereof she spoke, because for much of her early life she was estranged from the peace that Christ promises all who enter into oneness with Him. In *The Unselfishness of God,* written at age 70 near the end of her remarkable life, we learn that contrary to what some may believe, her journey was not one long uninterrupted, unquestioning, pain-free walk of faith. Like all of us, she had her doubts and trials, her losses and disappointments, her valleys as well as mountaintops. But what seems to have made her pilgrimage so successful was a penchant to prove, rather than disprove, God's proclamations and promises—and she insisted on proving them herself.

One thing she would not countenance was a second-hand faith. Her feisty passion for spiritual truth and wisdom caused her to reject pat answers and canned prescriptions with dispatch. A "birthright Quaker," Mrs. Smith recalls that there was no talk of "conversion" or being "born again" among her kith and kin, because they believed that their relationship with God was complete and whole from first breath.

Yet intuitively her heart told her that something more was required—some acknowledgment, some acceptance, some assent, some affirmation. Only, however, when circumstances exposed her to other Christian traditions (namely Plymouth Brethren and at Methodist holiness meetings) did she gain new understanding of what God asks of His children in response to Christ's sacrificial act.

A personal tragedy was also to figure in her spiritual awakening: the death of her five-year-old daughter. Up until then she writes, "I was struggling over my feelings, and never succeeded in making them what I thought they ought to be; and as a consequence my life was misery. But after I learned that the facts of religion were far more important than my feelings about these facts, I became happy in my religious life, and had without any effort, the very feelings of love to God and of rest and peace and joy in my soul that before I had so vainly tried to work up."

The question was not "How do I feel," she discovered, "but what does God say?" And then with insight wrapped in joy she concludes, "I had got hold of that which is the necessary foundation (of faith), namely reconcilation with God . . . All my fear of Him had vanished. He loves me, He forgave me, He was on my side and all was right between us . . . I had got my first glimpse of the unselfishness of God, only a glimpse but it was enough to make me radiantly happy."

Herein lies the central message of Mrs. Smith's faith story: the personal revelation that God is not an oppressive, self-centered tyrant, but an unconditionally loving and benevolent parent. From this breakthrough, Mrs. Smith recounts other major steps in her life-long adventure of faith—the pain and the gain. Though she does not dwell on her bumps and bruises, she had her share.

Still she persevered and with unflinching faith faced life's lengthening shadows with characteristic optimism. In her glorious concluding chapter on old age and death, she contemplates the splendor of heaven:

"I have had a few faint glimpses of this glory now and here," she says, "and it has been enough to ravish my heart. But there I shall see Him as He is, in all the glory of an infinite unselfishness which no heart of man has ever been able to conceive; and I await the moment with joy."

No wonder Hannah Whitall Smith was such a tremendous inspiration to people of her time; no wonder her words still ring with such undiminished power and majesty.

Fred Bauer
for the Publisher

INTRODUCTION

On the flyleaf of my Bible I find the following words, taken from I know not where: "This generation has rediscovered the unselfishness of God."

If I were called upon to state in one sentence the sum and substance of my religious experience, it is this sentence I would choose. And no words could express my thankfulness for having been born into a generation where this discovery has been comparatively easy.

If I am not mistaken, the generation before mine knew very little of the unselfishness of God; and, even of my own generation, there are I fear many good and earnest Christians who do not know it yet. Without putting it into such words as to shock themselves or others, many Christians still at bottom look upon God as one of the most selfish, self-absorbed Beings in the universe, far more selfish than they could think it right to be themselves,—intent only upon His own honor and glory, looking out continually that His own rights are never trampled on; and so absorbed in thoughts of Himself and of His own righteousness, as to have no love or pity to spare for the poor sinners who have offended Him.

I grew up believing God was like this. I have discovered that He is exactly the opposite. And it is of this discovery I want to tell.

After more than seventy years of life I have come to the profound conviction that every need of the soul is to be met by the discovery I have made. In that wonderful prayer of our Lord's in John 17, He says, "And this is life eternal, that they might know Thee the only true God, and Jesus Christ whom Thou hast sent." This used to seem to me a mystical saying, that might perhaps have a pious esoteric meaning, but certainly could have no practical application. But every year of my religious life I have discovered in it a deeper and more vital meaning; until now at last I see, that,

11

rightly understood, it contains the gist of the whole matter. To know God, as He really is, in His essential nature and character, is to have reached the absolute, and unchangeable, and utterly satisfying foundation, upon which, and upon which only, can be reared the whole superstructure of our religious life.

To discover that He is not the selfish Being we are so often apt to think Him, but is instead really and fundamentally unselfish, caring not at all for Himself, but only and always for us and for our welfare, is to have found the answer to every human question, and the cure for every human ill.

But how to make this discovery is the crucial question. In our present stage of existence we have not the faculties developed that would make it possible for us to see God as He is in His essential and incomprehensible Being. We need an Interpreter. We must have an Incarnation. If I should want to make a colony of ants know me as I am in the essential essence of my being, I would need to incarnate myself in the body of an ant, and speak to them in their own language, as one ant to another. As a human being I might stand over an ant-hill and harangue for a lifetime, and not one word would reach the ears of the ants. They would run to and fro unconscious of my speech.

To know God, therefore, as He really is, we must go to His incarnation in the Lord Jesus Christ. The Bible tells us that no man hath seen God at any time, but that the only begotten Son of the Father, He hath revealed Him. When one of the disciples said to Christ, "Show us the Father, and it sufficeth us," Christ answered—"have I been so long time with you, and yet hast thou not known me, Phillip? He that hath seen Me hath seen the Father, and how sayest thou then, Show us the Father? Believest thou not that I am in the Father, and the Father in Me? The words I speak unto you I speak not of Myself: but the Father that dwelleth in Me, He doeth the works."

Here then is our opportunity. We cannot see God, but we can see Christ. Christ was not only the Son of God, but He was the Son of man as well, and, as a man to men, He can reveal His Father. Whatever Christ was, that God is. All the unselfishness, all the tenderness, all the kindness, all the justice, all the goodness, that we see in Christ is simply a revelation of the unselfishness, the tenderness, the kindness, the justice, the goodness of God.

Some one has said lately, in words that seem to me inspired, "Christ is the human form of God." And this is the explanation of the Incarnation.

I do not mean, however, to say that no one can have any revelation of God to their souls except those who believe the Bible, and who know Christ as He is there revealed. I believe reverently and thankfully that "God is no respecter of persons: but in every nation, he that feareth Him and worketh righteousness is accepted with Him." God has "not left Himself without a witness" at any age of the world. But what I do believe is exactly what is declared in the opening words of the Epistle to the Hebrews, that God, who "at sundry times and in divers manners spake in times past to the Fathers by the Prophets, hath in these last days spoken unto us by His Son," who is the "brightness of His glory, and the express image of His person"; and that, therefore, although we may find many partial revelations elsewhere, if we would know Him as He really is, we can only see Him fully revealed in His "express image," the Lord Jesus Christ.

It was a long time before I found this out, and, until I did, I was, as my story will show, as really ignorant of Him as the most benighted savage, notwithstanding the fact that I lived in a Christian community, and was brought up in a Christian Church, and had the open Bible in my hand. God was a terror to me, until I began to see Him in the face of Jesus Christ, when He became an unmixed joy. And I believe many weary souls are in a similar case, who, if they could once be made to see that God is like Christ, would experience an unspeakable relief.

A friend of mine told me that her childhood was passed in a perfect terror of God. Her idea of Him was that He was a cruel giant with an awful "Eye" which could see everything, no matter how it might be hidden, and that He was always spying upon her, and watching for chances to punish her, and to snatch away all her joys. She said she would creep into bed at night with the dreadful feeling that even in the dark the "Eye of God" was upon her; and she would pull the bed covers over her head in the vain hope, which all the while she knew was vain, of hiding herself from this terrifying Eye, and would lie there in a tremble of fright, saying to herself in an agonized whisper, "What shall I do? Oh, what *shall* I do? Even my mother cannot save me from God!"

With a child's strange reticence she never told any one of her terror; but one night her mother, coming into the room unexpectedly, heard the poor little despairing cry, and, with a sudden comprehension of what it meant, sat down beside the bed, and, taking the cold little hand in hers, told her that God was not a dreadful tyrant to be afraid of, but was just like Jesus; and that she knew how good and kind Jesus was, and how He loved little children, and took them in His arms and blessed them. My friend said she had always loved the stories about Jesus, and when she heard that God was like Him, it was a perfect revelation to her, and took away her fear of God forever. She went about all that day saying to herself over and over, "Oh, I am so glad I have found out that God is like Jesus, for Jesus is so nice. Now I need never be afraid of God any more." And when she went to bed that night she fairly laughed out loud at the thought that such a dear kind Eye was watching over her and taking care of her.

This little child had got a sight of God "in the face of Jesus Christ," and it brought rest to her soul.

By the discovery of God, therefore, I do not mean anything mysterious, or mystical, or unattainable. I simply mean becoming acquainted with Him as one becomes acquainted with a human friend; that is, finding out what is His nature, and His character, and coming to understand His ways. I mean in short discovering what sort of a Being He really is—whether good or bad, whether kind or unkind, whether selfish or unselfish, whether strong or weak, whether wise or foolish, whether just or unjust.

It is of course evident that everything in one's religious life depends upon the sort of God one worships. The character of the worshiper must necessarily be molded by the character of the object worshiped. If it is a cruel and revengeful God, or a selfish and unjust God, the worshiper will be cruel, and revengeful, and selfish, and unjust, also. If it is a loving, tender, forgiving, unselfish God, the worshiper will be loving, and tender, and forgiving, and unselfish, as well. Also the peace and happiness of the worshiper must necessarily be absolutely bound up in the character of the God worshiped; for everything depends upon whether He is a good God or a bad God. If He is good, all is well of course, and one's peace can flow like a river; while, if He is bad, nothing can be well, no matter how earnest or devoted the worshiper may be, and no peace is possible.

This was brought very vividly to my mind by hearing once in a meeting an educated Negro, belonging to one of the tribes of Africa, giving an account of their religion.

He said that they had two gods, a good god and a bad god; that they did not trouble themselves about the good god, because, as he was good, he would do right anyhow, whether they sacrificed to him or not; but the bad god they had to try and propitiate by all sorts of prayers, and sacrifices, and offerings, and religious ceremonies, in order, if possible, to get him into a good humor, so that he might treat them well. To my thinking, there was a profound truth in this. The poorer and more imperfect is one's conception of God, the more fervent and intense will be one's efforts to propitiate Him, and to put Him into a good humor; whereas on the other hand, the higher and truer is the knowledge of the goodness and unselfishness of God, the less anxiety, and fuss, and wrestling, and agonizing, will there be in one's worship. A good and unselfish God will be sure to do right anyhow, whether we try to propitiate Him or not, and we can safely trust Him to carry on His affairs with very little advice from us. As to wrestling or agonizing with Him to fulfill what are really only the duties of His position, it could never be necessary; for, of course a good person always does his duty.

I have discovered therefore that the statement of the fact that "God is good," is really, if we only understand it, a sufficient and entirely satisfactory assurance that our interests will be safe in His hands. Since He is good, He cannot fail to do His duty by us, and, since He is unselfish, He must necessarily consider our interests before His own. When once we are assured of this, there can be nothing left to fear.

Consequently the only really vital thing in religion is to become acquainted with God. Solomon says, "Acquaint thyself with God, and be at peace"; and I believe every one of us would find that a peace that passes all understanding must necessarily be the result of this acquaintance.

Who is there on earth who could see and know the goodness, and the kindness, and the justice, and the loving unselfishness, of our God, as he is revealed to us in the face of Jesus Christ, and fail to be irresistibly drawn to adore Him? Who could have anything but peace in coming to know that the God who has created us, and to whom we belong forever, is a God of Love? Who of us can have any more fears, after once we have found out that He cares for us as for the apple of His eye? And what else is there that can bring an unwavering peace? Acquaintance with doctrines or dogmas may give peace for a time, or blissful experiences may, or success in service; but the peace from these can never be trusted to abide. Doctrines may become obscure, experiences may be dulled or may change, we may be cut off by providential circumstances from our work, all things and all people may seem to fail us; and unless our peace is founded upon something more stable than any of these, it will waver as the waves of the sea. The only place therefore of permanent and abiding peace is to be found in an acquaintance with the goodness and the unselfishness of God.

It is difficult to explain just what I mean by this acquaintance with God. We are so accustomed to think that knowing things *about* Him is sufficient—what He has done, what He has said, what His plans are, and what are the doctrines concerning Him,—that we stop short of that knowledge of what He really is in nature and character, which is the only satisfactory knowledge.

In human relations we may know a great deal about a person without at all necessarily coming into any actual acquaintance with that person; and it is the same in our relations with God. We may blunder on for years thinking we know a great deal about Him, but never quite sure of what sort of a Being He actually is, and consequently never finding any permanent rest or satisfaction. And then, perhaps suddenly, we catch a sight of Him as He is revealed in the face of Jesus Christ, and we discover the real God, as He is, behind, and beneath, and within, all the other conceptions of Him which may have heretofore puzzled us; and from that moment our peace flows like a river, and in everything and through everything, when perhaps we can rejoice in nothing else, we can always and everywhere "rejoice in God, and joy in the God of our Salvation." We no longer just need His promises; we have found Himself, and He is enough for every need.

My own experience has been something like this. My knowledge of God, beginning on a very low plane, and in the midst of the greatest darkness and ignorance, advanced slowly through many stages, and with a vast amount of useless conflict and wrestling, to the place where I learned at last that Christ was the "express image" of God, and where I became therefore in a measure acquainted with Him, and discovered to my amazement and delight His utter unselfishness, and saw that it was safe to trust Him. And from this time all my doubts and questionings have been slowly but surely disappearing in the blaze of this magnificient knowledge.

It is of the processes leading to this discovery by my own soul that I want to tell. But in order to do this I must begin with the earliest influences of my life, for I am convinced that my knowledge of my Heavenly Father began first of all in my knowledge of my earthly father and mother, who were, I feel sure, the most delightful father and mother any child ever had. Having known them and their goodness, it was only reasonable for me to believe that my Heavenly Father, who had made them, must be at least as good as the earthly father and mother He had made; and no story of my soul would be complete without beginning with them.

CHAPTER ONE

MY PARENTS

I was born in Philadelphia, Pennsylvania, in the year 1832. My parents were strict Quakers, and until my marriage at nineteen, I knew nothing of any other religion. I had an absolutely happy childhood and girlhood. I think so now, as I look back upon it, and my diary, kept from the time I was sixteen years old, shows that I thought so then. One of my first entries made in 1848 was as follows:—

> "Sixteen years of my life have passed, and, as I look back at the bright and happy days of my childhood, and at the quieter but more earnest enjoyments of my youth, my heart feels almost bursting with gratitude to my kind and gracious Creator who has filled my cup of joy almost to overflowing. Truly my life has been one fairy scene of sunshine and of flowers."

This may seem a very roseate view to take of one's life, and might be set down to the enthusiasm and glamour of youth. But on looking back now at seventy years of age, I can still say the same.

Under the date of 7/10/1849, when I was seventeen years old I wrote:

"I cannot understand it. I have thought that unless trials and afflictions come to wean me from the joys of this life, I shall never seek the higher and holier joys of Heaven. But instead of afflictions, every day my blessings increase. All around me conduces to my happiness; the world is very beautiful, my friends are the loveliest and kindest that any one ever had; and scarcely a trial or vexation comes to cast a cloud over my pathway. And this happiness, this Fate of happiness, I might almost call it, extends even to the smallest circumstances. Whatever I leave to God to decide for me He always decides just as I want Him to. . . . There is a continual clapping of hands and shouting of joyful voices in my heart, and every breath feels almost as if it must terminate in a smile of happiness. Mother says I laugh too much, but the laugh is in me, and will come out, and I cannot help it."

The same year under the date of 12/29 I wrote:

"What a happy, happy home is ours. I could not but think of it today as the merry jokes and tones of heartfelt pleasure echoed around our family board. And this evening, too, as we gathered together in our simple but comfortable parlour, it came over me with a perfect throb of joy. Father was sitting on one end of a sofa leaning his head on one hand, with the other hand resting on mother's lap; she sat next, and my head was in her lap, and I occupied the rest of the sofa, I have no doubt, gracefully and well. Sallie was sitting in a chair at the end of the sofa leaning her head on father's shoulder, and Lop-no-Nose (My sister Mary) was seated at all our feet, leaning first on one and then on another. All of us were talking as hard as we could, and feeling as if there was nothing wanting, but our absent, dearly loved brother Jim, to make our happiness complete. Many perhaps would smile at such quiet, unobtrusive pleasures, but for my part they are the kind of pleasures I enjoy most heartily and entirely. We can never weary of them, nor feel that their first beauty has gone, but each succeeding day makes them deeper and more earnest. Perhaps I am weak and foolish to take so much enjoyment in things which so many laugh at as unworthy of thought. I know I am but a child, and pleased, as children are, with very little things. And yet to me they are not little. A few of my father's pleasant jokes, spoken when I am brushing his hat or coat in the morning, will fill my heart with sunshine for a whole day. And I am happy if I may read aloud to my mother some book which I love, or even if I may sit quite still and think. Oh, I do love my home better than any other place I know of! I wonder if I love it too much. Sometimes I fear I do, for even if I leave it for one night I am more homesick than I would like any one to know, except those for whom I long. Even when I simply take a walk I often almost feel as if I could cry to go home again. It is very foolish, but I cannot help it. I should die if I had no one to love, no home!

"But for one thing, and I would be *perfectly* happy,—a father and mother, dearer, nobler far, than I can express, a brother and sisters, uncles and aunts, and cousins, and friends, all to love me, and, better far, all for me to love—with these priceless blessings I could not but be happy. One thing I say, prevents it, but it prevents it only a very little. It is the knowledge that I am not prepared for eternity, and the small prospect I have that I ever shall be. I wish it would give me more uneasiness, and that I might feel the urgent necessity there is for me to act. But I cannot compel myself to feel it, and so I go on as careless and indifferent as though I had not the eternal salvation of my soul resting upon me. I know it is very dangerous, but I really can do nothing towards rousing myself; and so, in spite of it, I am happy—happy in myself, happy in my home—my own dear home, happy in my parents, my brother and sisters, and my friends, happy in this beautiful world in which I am placed—in short, happy everywhere and in everything,—thank God!"

In 1850, when I was eighteen, under date 4/25, I write:

"I have been thinking to-day of my present life, and I could hardly find words to express its happiness. Relatives, friends, circumstances, all are nearly perfect. Outwardly I have scarcely anything to wish for, unless it is for plenty of money to give away, and to buy flowers with. I am crowned with blessings every day and all the day long. Oh, there never was any one so blessed! . . . Everything is so beautiful, and everybody is so lovely, and I can enjoy it, and do enjoy it all to the very full. Sometimes I have such heart gushes, as I call them, that I can scarcely contain myself. I love them dearly, and yet after all perhaps they are a little foolish. They are caused by such slight things—a blade of grass, a leaf waving in the wind, a bright happy golden dandelion, even an old barrel, or a heap of stones, or the creaking of a shoe, often the rattling of a cart, or some equally common sound, give me for the moment a sense of most exquisite happiness. Why, I cannot tell. It is not the beauty of the sight nor the harmony of the sound, but only a something, I know not what, that causes my heart to gush up joyfully, and my very soul to expand. I sometimes think it must be association; but with what? I do not love creaking shoes nor rattling carts, and yet often when walking along the street I fairly laugh from inward pleasure at the something in that creaking or rattling. It is not so always. A hundred carts may rattle, and a hundred barrels or heaps of stones may be around me, and jar painfully on ear and eye; but once in a while comes *the one*, and then comes the heart gush. To-day a drop of rain fell on my forehead, and I could have laughed aloud. But it was very silly; and I am a foolish child altogether, and fear I always shall be. . . . Yesterday we went with mother to the Shelter (a home for little colored orphans). It was all very interesting there, but nothing pleased me so much as when the little Blackies repeated 'Sparkle, sparkle, water pure, dirty hands I can't endure,' with all the same gestures and motions I used so often to do myself at the 'Infant School.' That gave me a right earnest heart-gush. I seemed almost to see myself in short frocks and panties, a little white apron, and one of those (as we thought) inimitable nets with a beautiful bow on the side, which mother used to think was almost too gay, enclosing my frisky hair, sitting on the highest bench of all in the school, and feeling, and no doubt looking, as proud as a queen."

Again under date 7/9/1850, (after describing the pleasure of a little trip away from home):

"And yet the pleasantest of all was to get home again last night. Home is home, and there is no place like unto it. Every day I enjoy it more and more, and every day I am happier. Last night I felt too happy almost. I fairly wanted to turn heels over head in my exuberance, and I did scream with delight.

And all for no particular reason; only the influences around me were so beautiful, and it seemed just then so glorious to live—to live, and suffer patiently, and work earnestly and nobly, and trust cheerfully, for years and years, until the glorious end shall come and bring the reward of peace and everlasting happiness."

Later in the same year I write under date of 7/16:

"In two weeks we start for a journey through the New England States and to Newport. It is grand, this plan of going to Newport—just the very place I had set my heart on visiting this summer, though I did not at all expect it. But somehow, I can scarcely tell how, whenever I set my heart on anything I am nearly always gratified. From a child it has been so. I can scarcely remember being ever much disappointed, and I am sure every step of my life hitherto has been through sunshine and flowers. But I do not wonder, with such kind and good parents it could not be otherwise. They really could not do more than they do to make us happy, and they succeed beautifully. . . . I believe I do not know any children who have so many enjoyments clustered in their home, although I know many whose parents are far richer."

I might multiply these extracts almost indefinitely, for my diaries up to the age of nineteen are, with the exception of my religious struggles, which seemed very tragic, but did not really affect my spirits much, one long jubilant song of happiness. At nineteen I married, and a new life began for me, which had its own more mature joys; but girlhood was over, and its simple girlish "Fate of happiness," as I called it, was exchanged for the woman's life of sober responsibilities, and weighty, although delightful, cares.

In looking back now I can see that this "Fate of happiness" was created by two causes,—my health and my parents. As to health, I never knew, through all the first eighteen years of my life, except once when I had an attack of bilious fever, what it was to be even ailing. I never had a headache, I did not know I had a back, I never got tired, I had a perfect digestion, and nothing ever caused me the loss of a single hour's sleep. Moreover I was blessed with what people nowadays call *"la joie de vivre,"* and simply to live seemed often happiness enough for me.

But the chiefest charm of my life was that I possessed the most delightful father and mother that ever lived. In the narrow Quaker circle into which I was born, very few of the opportunities for amusement or excitement that come to young people nowadays, were open to us, and all the fun we could extract from life was of the most simple and innocent kind. But with such a father and mother as ours, no outside pleasures were needed. They were so sympathetic and loving, and so entirely on our side under all circumstances, that we looked upon them, not as uncomfortable criticizing "grownups," but almost as children like ourselves, with the same tastes and interests as our own. We considered them far better comrades than any others we knew; and no fun the world ever had to offer was half so attractive to us as a quiet talk with our mother, or a good game of romps with our fun-loving father.

They often used to say that they wanted their children to have a happy childhood "tucked under their jackets"; for they were sure it would make us better men and women, and they took care that we should have this priceless boon. In looking back it seems to me that there were absolutely no clouds over my childhood's sky. One of the much-amused young people of the present day said to me once, with rather an accent of pity, "It seems to me you did not have many amusements when you were young." "We did not need to," was my prompt reply. "We had our father and mother, and they were all the amusements we needed. They made our lives all sunshine."

I wish I could give to others the vivid pictures I have of their inexpressible delightfulness. We knew, down to the very bottom of our hearts, that they were on our side against the whole world, and would be our champions in every time of need. No one could oppress us, neither playmates, nor friends, nor enemies, not even our teachers (those paid oppressors of children, as we felt all teachers to be), nor any one the whole world over, without having to reckon with those dear champions at home; and the certain conviction of this, surrounded us with such a panoply of defense that nothing had power to trouble us overmuch. "We will tell father," or "We will tell mother," was our unfailing resource and consolation in every sorrow. In fact, so sure was I of their championship, that, when any of my friends or school fellows were in trouble, I used to say, "Oh well, never mind, come home with me and let us tell my father and mother"; feeling sure that that dear father and mother could set the whole world straight, if the chance were only given them. And when the answer would come, as it often did, "Oh, that would be of no use, for your father and mother cannot do everything," I would say, with a profound pity for their ignorance, "Ah, you do not know my father and mother!"

One of my sisters remembered to her dying day, with a deep sense of gratitude, a deliverance our father gave her from an oppressively long lesson before she was six years old. Kindergartens were not invented then, and all children were required to study abstract lessons in a way that would be considered almost inhuman in these days. My sister was toiling over a sum with a hopeless sense of incapacity, and with tears trickling over her cheeks, when my father entered the room and said: "Ho, Liney, what is going wrong?" She told him as well as she could, and she says she could never forget his tone of absolute comprehension and sympathy as he said, "Why, of course it is too hard for my little Sally Dimple; but never mind, put it away, and I will make it all right with thy teacher." And my sister says so strong a conviction came to her at that moment of her father's championship, that she went through all the rest of her school life with an absolute sense of protection that made it impossible for any "hard lessons" ever to trouble her again.

It was not that our father or mother encouraged us to shirk any duty that they felt we were capable of performing. But they had so much sympathy with us, and such a sense of real justice in their dealings with us, that they seemed always able to discriminate between the possible and the impossible, and to protect us from the latter, while cheerily stimulating our efforts after the former. They never took it for granted, as so many "grown-ups" do, that, because we were children, we must necessarily be in the wrong; but they judged the case on its own merits. I believe it was this certainty of their justice that was more of a steady comfort to us than almost anything else; and I am very sure it has helped me to understand the perfect justice of my Heavenly Father in a way I could not otherwise have done.

As I say, they always stimulated us to all right effort, but this was never by commands or by harsh scolding, but always by sympathy and encouragement. They recognized our individuality, and respected it, giving us principles for our guidance rather than many burdensome rules. As far as possible they threw the responsibility of our conduct upon ourselves. This degree of personal liberty was a necessity to my freedom-loving nature. Under any other *regime* I should have wilted and withered; or else, which I think is more likely, should have openly rebelled. But as it was, no matter how averse I might be to any task, or how discouraged at any difficulty, my father's cheery voice repeating one of his homely proverbs, "Come, come, Han, stand up to the rack, fodder or no fodder," would always drive away all my reluctance; and discouragements melted like snow before the sun, in the face of his courage-giving assertion, "What man has done, man can do, and" (he would slyly add) "consequently woman." No child could have withstood such inspiring courage.

My father's own life had been a living illustration of the courage that he so continually tried to instill into us. When a boy of sixteen, his father lost a large part of his fortune in some West Indian transactions, and his sons were obliged to do what they could for their own support. My father, with his adventurous spirit, chose the sea, and, beginning in the lowest place, he so rapidly worked his way upward, that at the early age of twenty-four, he was made captain of an East Indiaman, at that time the largest ship in the port of Philadelphia; and his voyages in this ship were remarkably successful. He always attributed his success to the care and guidance of his Heavenly Father, upon whom he relied in all his affairs, and whose especial help he always asked and believed he always received, in every time of need. At the age of twenty-nine he gave up the sea, and went into business in Philadelphia, and here the same energy and the same reliance upon Divine help so prospered him, that he was able to make a comfortable competence for his declining years.

I well remember when I was a little girl often wondering what sort of a boy my father had been, and deciding, as I watched the roguish twinkles in the corners of his clear grey eyes and the curves of fun around his genial mouth, that he must have been a perfectly splendid boy, and just the kind I would have liked for a playmate. For, getting on towards middle age as he was when we were young, we found him the best playmate we children ever had. Some of his old friends, who remembered him as a boy, used to tell us that he was at once the most provoking and the best beloved boy in all their circle. No one could keep their anger against him for more than a moment. Let his tricks be as vexatious as they might,—and he was, they say, full and brimming over with mischief all the day long—no anger could withstand his genuine and openly expressed sorrow at any trouble he may have caused, and the hearty and generous restitution he was always ready to offer, nor the merry rebound of fun that would burst out the moment his apologies had been accepted. He was always the first to help in every case of need; and every one, whether friend or foe, knew they could rely on him for any service he was capable of performing. All his friends loved and admired him, even while they scolded him, and they generally found themselves laughing at the very moment when they meant to be the most severe and frowning. From childhood to old age this power of winning love and approval continued with him; and the fun of his boyhood, developing into the genial merriment of the chastened Christian heart, gave his mature character a nameless charm.

In fact I do not believe there ever was a more contagiously cheerful being than our father. No one could help feeling happier because of his presence. His very handshake was an uplift, and seemed somehow to make the world brighter than it was before, and to put you in a better humor with yourself and with everyone around you. Many of my friends have told me that they would rather have had a handshake from him than receive a valuable gift from another man, because somehow, in that handshake, his heart seemed to go right to their hearts, with power to cheer and help. I remember well how, when my childhood's sky would be all darkened by some heavy childish affliction, a cheery "Well, Broadie," in his hearty voice, or some little passing joke spoken with a roguish twinkle of his loving grey eyes, would clear my sky in a moment, and make life all sunshine again. And, even when I was older, his power to cheer grew no less, and it was quite my habit, whenever I found myself down in the depths, to put myself somewhere in his way, with the certainty that even a moment's peep at his strong cheery face would lift me out. I can even remember that, in his absence, the sight and feel of his dear old overcoat would somehow brighten everything, and send me off encouraged to be braver and stronger. To make life happier for every one with whom he came in contact seemed to be his aim and his mission, and rarely has any one succeeded so well. Some one said to me, many years after his death, that "John M. Whitall was the best loved man in Philadelphia"; and in certain circles I am sure this was true.

Our mother also was equally well beloved. She was a most delightful mother, not so full of fun perhaps as our father, but always ready to champion her children's cause everywhere and at all times, and an unfailing rock of refuge to us in every emergency. Sweetness and goodness, purity and truth, seemed to emanate from her gracious presence; and, for every one who came in contact with her, she was an inspiration to all that was noble and good.

People talk in these days of an atmosphere surrounding each one of us, something like the nimbus that is always painted about the heads of saints. They say it seems to envelop the whole figure, and that it influences for good or evil all who come near it. It is called the "aura," and is the outcome of each one's character and inmost personality. Some auras, we are told, are dark and gloomy, and exert a depressing or even a wicked influence, while others are rose color, or gold, or opal, or sky blue and full of light, and their influence is cheering and uplifting; and all this without perhaps a word being said in either case. If this theory is true I feel sure that my father and mother possessed "auras" full of heaven's own sunshine, and, without knowing the reason, their children lived in perpetual cheer.

That a childhood so lived could not fail to have an enormous influence on the after history of any soul, seems to me incontrovertible; and I attribute my final satisfying discovery of my Heavenly Father largely to what I had known of the goodness of my earthly parents. They never said much about religion, for the Quaker fear of meddling between a soul and its Maker had created a habit of reserve that could not easily be broken through, but they showed plainly that their lives were lived in a region of profound faith in an ever-present God. We could not but see that He was to them a reality beyond all other realities. Of religious teaching we had but little, but of religious example and influence we had a never-failing supply. Not by talking, but by daily living, were impressions made on our childish hearts.

I remember once however when my father did speak out of the fullness of his heart, and when what he said made a profound and lasting impression upon me. I was a very imaginative child, and consequently very frightened of the dark, which I peopled with all sorts of terrible monsters, lurking under beds or behind doors, ready to rush out and devour me at any moment. Of course, with the profound reticence of childhood, I never spoke of this; but somehow my father at last found out that I was afraid of the dark, and instead of ridiculing my fears or scolding me, as I felt in my poor foolish little heart I deserved for making such a row, he took me lovingly on his knee, and, putting his dear strong arm around me, he said, in tones of the most profound conviction, "Why, Han, did thee not know there is never anything to be afraid of? Did thee not know that thy Heavenly Father is always with thee, and that *of course* He will always take care of thee?" And as I still trembled and shivered, he added, as though surprised that there could be any one in the world who did not know this, "I thought of course thee knew this, child." I never shall forget the profound impression this made upon me, nor the immediate and permanent relief from fear it gave me; and I have always been sure that this one statement of a fact, which was to my father the most tremendous reality of his life, has had more than anything else to do with the satisfying sense of God's presence which has for so long been my portion. It was not a religious dogma my father stated on this, to me, memorable occasion, but it was a simple, incontrovertible fact which he was surprised I did not know; and, as being the statement of a fact, it was far more comforting than any amount of preaching or arguing could possibly have been. God was with me—and that was enough; for of course, being with me, He would naturally take care of me. I remember that when my father lifted me down from his lap and told me cheerily to run along and not to be frightened any more, I walked off in a stately sort of way, feeling as if somehow I was safe inside an invisible fortress where I could laugh to scorn all the lurking monsters of the dark, and could hear their angry rustles unmoved.

I dare say the rarity of any direct religious teaching from our parents helped to make the few occasions when they did speak more impressive; but, however this may be, I can truly say that, though often obscured for a time, the convictions of that occasion have always been with me at bottom, and thousands of times in my life since, my father's words then, have brought me help.

CHAPTER TWO

MY QUAKER CHILDHOOD

*N*ext to the influence of my parents upon my young life, was the influence of the religious Society of which I was a birth-right member. I do not think it would be possible for me to express in words how strong and all pervading this influence was. Every word and thought and action of our lives was steeped in Quakerism. Never for a single moment did we escape from it. Not that we wanted to, for we knew nothing different; but, as my narrative will show, every atom of our consciousness was infused and possessed with it. Daily I thank God that it was such a righteous and enno-bling influence.

But, though so all-powerful in our lives, the Quakerism of my day did not achieve its influence by much outward teaching. One of its most profound beliefs was in regard to the direct inward teaching of the Holy Spirit to each individual soul; and this discouraged much teaching by human lips. The Quakers accepted as literally true the declarations of the Apostle John that there is a "true Light which lighteth every man that cometh into the world"; and their fundamental teaching was that this "Light," if faithfully looked for and obeyed, would lead every man into all truth. They felt therefore that it would be an interference between the soul and its Divine Guide and Teacher to intrude with any mere teaching of man. They taught us to listen for and obey the voice of God in our souls, and they believed if we did this up to our best knowledge, our Divine Guide would teach us all it was necessary for us to know of doctrines or dogmas.

There was something grand in this recognition of human individuality. It left each soul in an absolute independence before its Creator, ready to be taught directly by Him, without the interference of any human being, except as that human being might be inspired by Himself. And although in my youthful days I did not consciously formulate this, yet the atmosphere it created, and the individual dignity with which it endowed every human soul, whether wise or simple, rich or poor, learned or unlearned, old or young, made each of us feel from our earliest days a royal interior independence that nobody, not even our parents, could touch.

When the Bible was read to us, which was frequently done, especially on "First Day" afternoons, very little explanation was ever attempted but instead a few moments of profound silence were always observed at the close of the reading, in order that the "Inward Light" might, if it should be the Divine Will, reveal to us the meaning of what had been read. I am afraid however that personally I was still too unawakened for much ever to be revealed to me. But so strong was this feeling among the Quakers in my day, that direct religious teaching from the lips of human beings, except in inspired preaching, always seemed to me to be of the world, worldly, and I felt it was good only for the "world's people," who, because of their ignorance regarding the inward light, were necessarily obliged to look outward for their teaching. In fact all Bible expositions, except such as might be directly inspired, were felt to be worldly; and Bible classes and Sunday-schools were considered to be places of worldly amusement, which no true Quaker ought to attend. Our teaching was to come to us, not from the lips of human teachers, but from the inward voice of the Divine Teacher Himself.

In this the early Friends only believed what Saint Augustine taught when he said: "It is the inward Master that teacheth, it is the inspiration that teacheth; where the inspiration and unction are wanting, it is vain that words from without are beaten in."

Their preaching therefore was mostly composed of exhortations to listen for this "inward voice," and to obey it, when heard; and never once, during all my young days, do I remember hearing any other sort of preaching.

Not that there might not have been, however, doctrinal preaching as well, had I had the ears to hear it; but as a fact no religious questions of any sort, except the one overpowering conviction that somehow or other I must manage to be good, occupied my mind up to the age of sixteen. I lived only in that strange mysterious world of childhood, so far removed from the "grown-up world" around it, where everything outside seemed only a mere passing show. In my world all was plain and simple, with no need for any questionings. The grown-up people around me seemed to have their ridiculous interests and their foolish bothers, but these were nothing to me in my enchanted sphere. Sometimes, when one of these silly grown-ups would suggest that a time would come when I also would be grown up, a pang would come over me at the dreadful thought, and I would resolve to put off the evil day as long as possible, by refusing to have my hair done up in a knot behind, or to have my dresses come below my knees. I had an idea that grown up people wanted to live children's lives, and play children's plays, and have children's fun, just as much as we children did, but that there was a law which forbade it. And when people talked in my presence about the necessity of "taking up the cross" as you grew older, I thought they meant that you would have to stop climbing trees or rolling hoops, or running races, or walking on the tops of fences, although all the while you would want to do these things as much as ever; and my childish heart was often filled with a profound pity for the poor unfortunate grown-ups around me.

I was a wild harum-scarum sort of being, and up to the age of sixteen was nothing but a light-hearted, irresponsible child, determined to get all the fun I could out of life, and with none of the morbid self-consciousness that is so often such a torment to young people.

The fact was, as far as I can recollect, I scarcely ever thought of myself, as myself, at all. My old friends tell me now that I was considered a very pretty girl, but I never knew it. The question as to my looks never occurred to me. The only question that really interested me was as to my fun; and how I looked, or what people thought of me were things that did not seem in the least to concern me.

I remember distinctly the first time such questions intruded themselves, and the indignant way in which I rejected them. I think I must have been about eleven years old. My mother had sent for me to go into the drawing-room to see some of her friends who had asked for me. Without a fear I left my lessons, and went towards the drawing-room; when suddenly, just as I was about to enter, I was utterly surprised and taken aback by an attack of shyness. I had never had the feeling before, and I found it most disagreeable. And as I turned the door-knob I said to myself, "This is ridiculous. Why should I be afraid of those people in there? I am sure they won't shoot me, and I do not believe they will think anything about me; and, even if they do, it can't hurt, and I simply *will not* be frightened." And as I said this, I deliberately threw my shyness behind my back, and walked fearlessly into the room, leaving it all outside the door. I had made the discovery, although I did not know enough then to formulate it, that shyness was simply thinking about oneself, and that to forget oneself was a certain cure; and I do not remember ever really suffering from shyness again. If it ever came, I just threw it behind me as I had done the first time, and literally refused to pay any attention to it.

As far as I can remember therefore my life, up to the age of sixteen, when my religious awakening came, was an absolutely thoughtless child's life. Self-introversion and self-examination were things of which I knew nothing, and religious questions were not so much as dreamed of by me. I look back with wonder that so thoughtless a being could have been so preserved from outbreaking sin as I was, but I recognize that for this I must thank the grand all-enveloping Quaker atmosphere of goodness and righteousness, in which I lived, and which made any such outbreaks almost an impossibility.

I have spoken of the Church into which I was born as a religious society. It was always called in my young days, "The religious Society of Friends," and was never by any chance spoken of, as it often is now, as "The Quaker Church." The early Quakers had a strong testimony against calling themselves a Church, for they did not consider themselves a Church in any exclusive or inclusive sense of that word. The Church, according to their view, was the invisible body of all believers, belonging to every creed and every nation, and they as "Friends" were only a "Society" within this great universal invisible Church. They took their name from our Lord's words in John 15:14, 15: "Ye are My friends if ye do whatsoever I command you. Henceforth I call you not servants; for the servant knoweth not what his Lord doeth; but I have called you friends, for all things that I have heard of My Father I have made known unto you." Their one aim in life was to do whatsoever the Lord commanded, and they believed therefore that they had been admitted into this sacred circle of the Divine friendship. They had at first no idea of forming a separate sect, but their association was to their minds only a society of friends (with neither a capital *S* nor a capital *F*), who met together to share as friends, one with another, the Divine revelations that were made to each, and to encourage one another to strive after the righteousness that the Divine friendship demanded. That this "society of friends" gradually assumed a definite article and capital letters to itself, and became "The Religious Society of Friends," and developed into a separate sect, was, I suppose, the necessary outcome of all such movements, but it has always seemed to me a falling away from the simplicity and universality of the original idea.

The name of Quaker had been bestowed upon them in their early days from the fact that, when preaching in their Meetings, they were seen to quake or tremble under what they believed to be the power of the Holy Ghost. I myself, even in the quieter times when I was a child, would often see the preachers in our meetings trembling and quaking from head to foot, and I confess I always felt that messages delivered under this condition had a special inspiration and unction of their own, far beyond all others. In fact, unless a preacher had at least enough of this "quaking" to make their hearts palpitate and their legs tremble, they were not considered by many to have the real "call" to the ministry at all; and one cannot therefore be surprised that the name "Quaker" had fastened itself on the society.

But the name chosen by themselves was a far happier one, and far more descriptive of what they really were. The "quaking" was after all only an incident in their religion, but friendliness was its very essence. Because they believed themselves to be the friends of God, they realized that they must be in the truest sense the friends of all the creatures He had created. They believed it was literally true that He had made all the nations of men of one blood, and that all were therefore their brethren. One could not fail to realize this sense of universal friendship through all the worship and the work of the society; and personally, so deeply was it impressed upon my young life, that to this day to be a member of the Society of Friends means to me to be everybody's friend; and whenever there is any oppression or suffering anywhere in the world, I instinctively feel sure that among the first to hasten to the rescue will be a committee of the Society of Friends. They have in fact a standing Committee which meets regularly to consider cases of wrong and of need, and it is called significantly "The Meeting for Sufferings." The society is and always has been the friend of all who are oppressed.

Therefore, while the outside world generally calls them "Quakers," I am glad that they themselves have held steadfastly to the endearing name of "Friends."

CHAPTER THREE

QUAKERISM

*B*efore entering upon the subject of the influence of Quakerism on my young life, I want it to be thoroughly understood that I am not trying in any sense to give a true transcript of Quakerism, as my elders understood it and lived it, but only as it influenced an undeveloped eager girl, who had a decidedly religious side to her nature, but who was too full of life and spirits to be very seriously interested in any abstract questions outside of her everyday duties and fun.

I cannot trace back my notions to any definite teaching, and at the time I did not formulate them, but the impressions I retain of those days seem to me now to have had their rise in the general atmosphere that surrounded me. It is very likely that my adult relatives and friends had no idea of creating such an atmosphere, and, if they were alive now, would be very much surprised at some of my interpretations. But the fact remains that the Quakerism of my young life has left the strong impressions I record, and I want to give them as truthfully as I can, as part of my own personal history, and not at all as an authoritative exposition of Quaker views.

In tracing back the line of our ancestors, we find that they came over from England during the seventeenth century, in company with a great body of Quakers who, unable to find in their own land that spirit of religious liberty which was a fundamental article of their faith, sought an asylum in the new Western world, hoping there to found a state where their children might enjoy that freedom to worship God according to the dictates of their own consciences, which had been denied to themselves in the old world. These Quakers had settled largely in the colonies founded by William Penn in and around Philadelphia, on both sides of the Delaware River, and had become, by the time I was born, a most influential and respected body.

A good deal of their early freshness and fervor had however passed away, and it was a very sober, quiet sort of religion that remained, which allowed of but little expression, and was far more entirely interior than seems to me now to have been wise. There had been left from earlier days a firm belief in what was always spoken of as the "perceptible guidance of the Holy Spirit," meaning the distinct and conscious voice of God in the heart; and a loyal devotion to what were called "Friends' testimonies," which testimonies were the outward expression of the convictions of truth that had, they believed, been directly revealed by the "inward light" to George Fox, the founder of the society, and to his early followers.

Many of these convictions were opposed to the usual ideas of people around us, and their observance therefore made the Quakers of my day very peculiar. But we were taught that it was a great honor to be God's "peculiar people," and I for one fully believed that we Quakers were meant where it says in Deuteronomy, "The Lord hath chosen thee to be a peculiar people unto Himself above all the nations that are upon the earth." In the face of such an honor, the things in which we were "peculiar," which often, I acknowledge, caused us considerable embarrassment and even trial, seemed to be a sort of "hall-mark" of especial Divine favor; and, instead of being mortified over their peculiarities, the Quakers of my day were secretly proud of them, and of the singularity they caused. We Quaker children imbibed somewhat of this feeling, and when we walked along the streets in our quaint Quaker garb, and the street gamins called after us, as they often did "Quaker, Quaker, mash potato" we felt a sustaining sense of superiority, that took some of the sting out of the intended insult, and enabled us to call back with a fine scorn, as having far the best of the matter, "Dutchy, Dutchy,

Mash-pay-touchy!" If we were Quakers, they were perhaps the descendants of the early German, or, as they were called, "Dutch Redemptioners" who were servants of the first colonists; and at any rate we were determined they would know we thought they were. I remember that after my sisters and I had discovered this effective retort, we were able to silence most of our persecutors.

But it was sometimes very hard for us Quaker children to be obliged to take our share of persecution for "conscience sake," since it was the consciences of our elders and not our own; and, combined with our pride in being God's peculiar people, we also often had a sense of ostracism that I feel on looking back, we ought not to have been asked to endure. Still I have no doubt it imparted to our characters a sort of sturdy independence that was of real value to us in our after life, and I for one have always been thankful for the deliverance from the fear of man, and the indifference to criticism, that was, I am convinced, engendered in my spirit by these early persecutions for "conscience sake."

There was, as I have said, very little direct religious teaching to the young Quakers in my time. We were sometimes preached to in our meetings, when a Friend in the gallery would exhort the "dear young people" to be faithful to their Divine Guide; but no doctrines or dogmas were ever taught us; and, unless one was especially awakened in some way, none of the questions that exercise the minds of young people in the present day were even so much as dreamed of by the young people of my circle, at least so far as I knew; and a creature more utterly ignorant of all so-called religious truth than I was up to the age of sixteen, when my awakening came, could hardly be conceived of in these modern times. The whole religious question for me was simply as to whether I was good enough to go to heaven, or so naughty as to deserve hell. As to there being a "plan of salvation," or any such thing as "justification by faith," it was never heard of among us. The one vital point in our ideas of religion was as to whether or not we looked for and obeyed that "perceptible guidance" of the Holy Spirit, to which we were constantly directed; and the only definite teaching we received as to our religious life was comprised in "Friends' testimonies," and in the "queries" read and answered every month in the "monthly meetings for business" which were regularly held by every congregation of Quakers.

We had no Sunday-schools nor Bible classes; in fact, as I have said, these were considered to be a form of "creaturely activity" only to be excused in the "world's people" (by which we meant everybody who was not a Quaker), because they were in ignorance, as we believed, of the far higher teachings of the Holy Spirit which were our special inheritance. Neither did our Society teach us any regular prayers, for Friends believed they could only pray acceptably when moved by the Spirit to pray. As little children our parents had taught us a childish prayer, which we repeated every night after we were tucked up in bed before the last farewell kisses were given. But as we grew older, and our parents recognized more and more our individual independence, these nightly childish prayers were omitted, and the Quaker atmosphere as regards prayer gradually gained the ascendency; and in time I, at least, came to feel as if, because of my light-hearted carelessness and indifference, it was almost wrong for me to try to pray.

What this Quaker teaching about prayer was may be gathered from the following extract from the writings of Isaac Penington. He says, "Prayer is a gift. A man cannot pray when he will; but he is to watch and to wait, when the Father will kindle in him living breathings towards Himself." In consequence we knew no formal prayers, and were not even taught the Lord's prayer, and until I was a woman I actually did not know it by heart, and even to this day I am often puzzled for a moment when I try to repeat it. The real truth is that as a child I got the impression somehow that the Lord's prayer was frivolous and that only frivolous people were expected to use it. By frivolous we meant anything that was not Quakerly. Quakers were "plain" and all the rest of the world, and even of the Church were frivolous.

It even seemed to me that it was distinctly frivolous to kneel in prayer. We Friends always stood when prayer was offered in our meetings, and if we ever prayed on retiring at night, it was done after we got into bed. And when, as sometimes happened, one of our little circle ventured to kneel beside her bed for her evening devotions, we always felt that it was a lamentable yielding to a worldly spirit, and was to be mourned over as a backsliding from the true faith.

As a fact all Church or Chapel services seemed to us very gay and worldly, and to join in them seemed almost to amount to sinning; and until I was married I had actually never entered any place of worship other than Friends' Meeting houses. I should have felt it a distinct "falling from grace" to have done so.

I cannot remember that we were distinctly taught any of these things, or that any one ever said to me in so many words that Quakers were the "peculiar people" spoken of in the Bible as being especially dear to God; but the sort of preaching to which we listened, and only of course half understood, in regard to the privileges and the blessings of our peculiarities, made the impression upon my young ignorance that in some way, because of our "peculiarities," we were the objects of especial Divine favor; and I can remember very well having the distinct feeling that we were the true Israelites of whom the Bible spoke, and that all who where not Quakers belonged to the "outside Gentiles." To tell the whole truth I had as a child a confused idea in my mind that we Quakers had a different and a far higher God than others, and that the God other Christians worshiped was one of the "Gods of the Gentiles" whom the Bible condemned.

That I was not singular in these feelings will be shown in the following extracts from the lately published reminiscences of an American Friend, who is an able educationalist of the present day.[1] He says:

"I am quite sure no Israelite in the days of Israel's prosperity ever had a more certain conviction that he belonged to a peculiar people whom the Lord had chosen for His own, than I did. There was for me an absolute break between 'us' and anybody else. This phariseeism was never taught me, nor encouraged directly by anybody, but I none the less had it. If I had anything in the world to glory over it was that I was a Quaker. Others about me had a good deal more that was tangible than I had. Their life was easier, and they did not have as hard a struggle to get the things they wanted as we did. But they were not 'chosen,' and we were! As far back as I can travel in my memory I find this sense of superiority—a sort of birthright into Divine grace and favor. I think it came partly from impressions I got from 'traveling Friends,' whose visits had an indescribable influence upon me. It will of course seem to have been a very narrow view, and so it was, but its influence was decidedly important upon me. It gave somewhat of a dignity to my little life to feel that I belonged to God's own people; that, out of all the world, *we* had been selected to be

[1] "A Boy's Religion," by Rufus M. Jones.

His, and that His wonders had been worked for *us*, and *we* were objects of His special love and care.

"Everybody at home, as well as many of our visitors, believed implicitly in immediate divine guidance. Those who went out from our meeting to do extended religious service, and there were many such visits undertaken, always seemed as directly selected for these momentous missions, as were the prophets of old. As far back as I can remember, I can see Friends sitting talking with my grandmother of some 'concern' which was 'heavy upon them,' and the whole matter seemed as important as though they had been called by an earthly king to carry on the affairs of an empire. It was partly these cases of divine selection, and the constant impression that God was using these persons, whom I knew, to be His messengers, that made me so sure of the fact that we were His chosen people. At any rate I grew up with this idea firmly fixed."

I believe every young "Friend," in the circle to which I belonged, would have owned to the same feelings. We were God's "chosen people," and, as such, belonged to a religious aristocracy as real as any earthly aristocracy could be; and I do not believe any earl or duke was ever prouder of his earthly aristocratic position than we were of our heavenly one.

CHAPTER FOUR

QUAKER TRUTH AND QUAKER MINISTRY

*S*o certain were the "Friends" that theirs was the true faith set forth in the Bible and preached by the Apostles, that in speaking of it they always in my day called it the "Truth," with a capital "T," and spoke of the religious work of the society as the "service of Truth." And I remember that my father's horses and carriages were called "Truth's horses and carriages," because they were so continually in requisition to convey preachers from one meeting to another, or to do errands for the Elders or Overseers. With the unquestioning faith of childhood I fully believed all this, and grew up with a distinct idea that we "Friends" had practically a monopoly of "The Truth," with a strong emphasis on the definite article, which differentiated it entirely from the holding of one truth among many. Ours was the whole truth, and nothing but the truth, and could not be improved upon. Such was my idea in the days of my youth.

That "Friends" did, however, hold a great deal of truth (without any definite article) cannot be denied. Nearly every view of divine things that I have since discovered, and every reform I have since advocated, had, I now realize, their germs in the views of the Society; and over and over again, when some new discovery or conviction has dawned upon me, I have caught myself saying, "Why, *that* was what the early Friends meant, although I never understood it before."

Many of their great moral and religious principles have been gradually adopted and taught by other Christians—the use of the Sabbath for man, and not man for the Sabbath, the subordination of the symbol to the spiritual belief symbolized, the comparative unimportance of creeds and dogmas, or of rites and ceremonies, the abhorrence of slavery, the vital importance of temperance, the direct access of the soul to God without human intermediary. But in the day when the Quakers first declared these things, they seemed like hard sayings which only a few could bear. And even those of us who were brought up with them from our very cradles, needed many years of spiritual growth and enlightenment before we could fully comprehend them.

One of the truths they had got hold of far ahead of their time was in regard to the equality in the sight of God between men and women. They gave to their "women Friends" an equal place with "men Friends" in the work of the ministry, and in the government of the Society. There were women Preachers, and women Elders, and women Overseers, who sat in equal state with the men Preachers, and Elders, and Overseers, on the raised benches in solemn rows, facing the body of the meeting, the men on one side of the middle aisle, and the women on the other. The preachers, (or Ministers, as we called them), sat at the head of these solemn rows, the oldest and weightiest nearest the top, and gradually tapering down to the younger neophytes, whose gifts had only lately been "acknowledged."

The system of the ministry among Friends was very different from that of any other church. They believed profoundly that only God could make a Minister, and that no preaching was right except such preaching as was directly and immediately inspired by Him. They accepted, as the only true equipment for the work of the ministry, the declaration contained in Matthew 10:18-20, and they believed its promises would be literally fulfilled to every faithful soul, whether man or woman, young or old, learned or unlearned. "And ye shall be brought before governors and kings for My sake for a testimony against them and the Gentiles. But when they deliver you up take no thought how or what ye shall speak; for it shall be given you in that same hour what ye shall speak, for it is not ye that speak but the Spirit of your Father which speaketh in you." This promise contained for them the Quaker "Call" and the Quaker "Ordination"; and to "study for the ministry" in colleges or out of books, or to be ordained by the laying on of human hands, seemed to them the rejection of the only Divine call and ordination, and to result in what they termed a "man made ministry." In their view Ministers could be made only by God, and the power to preach was a direct "gift" bestowed by Him alone. All that could be done was for the Elders and Overseers of the meeting to watch the development of this gift; and, when it seemed to them that the speaking bore unmistakable signs of a Divine "unction," they would meet together and decide whether or not to record on their meeting-book that they "acknowledged" so and so to be a Minister. This act of "recording" or "acknowledging" did not make the speakers Ministers; it was only the recognition and acknowledgment of the fact that God had already made them such. When this had been done, they were called "acknowledged Ministers," and were felt by us young people to have been admitted into the hierarchy of heaven itself.

Moreover, since God had made them Ministers, their payment or remuneration must come from Him alone. No stipends or salaries were ever given them, but their ministry, freely bestowed from above, was freely handed forth to their fellow-members, without money and without price. Consequently all Quaker Ministers continued in their usual occupations while "exercising their gifts," living on their own incomes, or carrying on their usual trades or businesses. It often left them but little time for study or preparation; but, as no study or preparation was permitted, this was no drawback.

For not only was there to be no especial training for the ministry, but it was not thought right to make preparation for any particular service or meeting. "Friends" were supposed to go to their meetings with their minds a blank, ready to receive any message that the Holy Spirit might see fit to impart. None of them could tell beforehand whether the inspiration would or would not come to them; and the promise was clear that, should it come, it would be given them in that same hour what they should speak. All preparation for preaching therefore was felt to be a disloyalty to the Holy Spirit, and was called "creaturely activity," meaning that it was the creature in the individual, and not the Spirit of God, that had taken control. And no such preaching was ever felt to have that "unction of the Spirit" which was the Quaker test of all ministry. I have found in an old book of selections from Isaac Penington's writings the following concerning ministers, which clearly expressed the Quaker view.

> "It is not preaching things that are true which makes a true minister, but the receiving of his ministry from the Lord. The gospel is the Lord's which is to be preached, and it is to be preached in His power; and the ministers who preach it are to be endued with His power, and to be sent by Him. . . . He that will be a true Minister must receive both his gift, his ministry, and the exercise of both, from the Lord, and must be sure in his ministering to keep in the power. . . . He must wait in his several exercises, to be endued with matter and power from on high, before he opens his mouth in a testimony for the Lord."

With this view of preaching it can easily be understood that to "appear in the ministry," as it was quaintly expressed, would be felt by all to be, not only a very solemn step, but also a truly awful one. In my young days it was always referred to as "taking up the cross," and was looked upon as the supreme sacrifice a soul could make. It has always been hard for me to understand this feeling, as in my own personal experience preaching has been far more of a pleasure than a sacrifice. But probably this may have been because I have let in more or less of what the early Friends would call the "creature" into my ministry, and have not attributed quite such a high origin to my utterances. An old letter of my mother's concerning the "appearance in the ministry" of her brother, my Uncle John Tatum, will illustrate the state of feeling I have described. She is writing to her father and mother about a visit to this uncle, and says:

> "Have you heard of the sacrifice that dear brother John has lately made in yielding to what I believe has been a long-felt impression of duty, by giving up to appear in public testimony and supplication in their meetings. It is since we were there; but we were both particularly struck with the marks of exercise and humble devotedness that appeared in his daily walk and conversation. I hope we shall all be willing to yield him the strength of our tenderest sympathy, and to pray that he may be led, and guided, and kept in the right way. He does, I believe, feel often much alone. He said to me, 'Ah, my dear

sister, it has been an awful time with me lately, in which I have had to seek the fields and woods alone, and pray mightily for strength and preservation.'"

I cannot but think that it was a false view of Christian service that led the Friends to go through such conflicts over what nowadays is embraced as a glorious privilege. But all Quakerism in my day was more or less tinged with this ascetic spirit of sacrifice, and it was so entirely the customary way of regarding the matter that each new recruit to the ministry unconsciously fell into it. That some of them had now and then a glimpse into the privilege of service, is shown by an incident that occurred with this very Uncle John some years later. He was speaking with my brother about a "religious visit" he had lately paid to some neighboring Meetings, and, as they separated, he said in a very solemn and mournful tone, "So thou wilt see, dear James, what a heavy cross has been laid upon me." My brother expressed his sympathy, and they parted, going different ways. But in a moment or two my uncle walked hastily back, and touching my brother on the arm said, "I am afraid, dear James, that I conveyed a false impression in what I said about my ministry being a cross. Truth compels me to confess to thee that it is not a cross at all, but a very blessed and delightful privilege. I am afraid we preachers talk as we do about the cross in preaching, more from habit than from any reality."

Everything conspired however to make Quaker ministry a most mysterious and solemn affair to us young people. There was something indescribably enticing in the idea of the direct and immediate inspiration of our preachers. We seemed to be living, as it were, on the very verge of the spiritual world, where at any moment the veil might be lifted, and we might have some mystical revelation from the other side; and the eager longing yet solemn awe with which we watched and waited for these revelations could not, I feel sure, be comprehended by the present generation of young people, even though they should themselves be Quakers. An awe and mystery surrounded for us every "ministering Friend" whether man or woman, rich or poor, wise or simple; and this wholly apart from the personality of the Minister. It was due only and entirely to the fact that we believed Ministers to be the divinely chosen oracles to declare the mind of God, and that every word they might say was directly inspired, and was almost as infallible as the Bible itself. Consequently what any one of them might be "led" to say to oneself was a matter of the most vital importance, and the most profound belief. One of the greatest excitements of my young life therefore was the possibility of being at any moment personally preached to or prophesied about by some "ministering Friend."

CHAPTER FIVE

QUAKER OPPORTUNITIES

*F*riends in my days had a way of having what were called "Opportunities." What this word really meant, I suppose now, was that they had an opportunity to "relieve their minds" of some "message" that was burdening it. But in those days no such ordinary explanation of the word ever occurred to me, but an "Opportunity" seemed a most mysterious divinely appointed function, that was akin to a council in the court of Heaven itself; and the one longing yet fear of my young life was for some preacher to have an "Opportunity" with me. On such occasions the preacher was supposed to be divinely enabled to see into your most secret thoughts, and to uncover with an unsparing hand the secret sins which you had fondly hoped were known to yourself alone. They were also supposed to be endowed with the power of reading the future, and might be expected to foretell any great blessings or dire misfortunes that were in store for you. The excitement, therefore, when a "traveling Friend" came to the house and asked for an "Opportunity" was intense. Whether fear or hope as to the revelations that might be made, predominated, it would be hard to say; but, no matter what our feelings might be, no member of the family, not even the smallest servant, might dare to be absent. In fact, when now and then circumstances appeared to make it desirable that some one should stay away, the preacher often seemed to have a sense of it, and would ask solemnly if there was no one else, and would decline to go on with the "Opportunity" until the absent one was summoned.

In these "Opportunities" the preacher was expected to "speak to the condition" of especial ones present, and the great excitement was as to whether one's own condition would be spoken to. With what eager hope and fear I always waited to see if the preacher would speak to *my* condition, no words can describe; but never once in my recollection was this supreme favor conferred upon me. No preacher ever vouchsafed to notice me in any especial manner, nor seemed aware of the presence of an eager hungry soul reaching blindly out after the Light, to whom a few words "direct from God" would have come as an unspeakable boon. To tell the truth I was always expecting some wonderful prophecy to be made concerning me—that I was to be a great preacher, and was to do some great work for God; and though I dreaded the revelations of my unrighteous condition that might be made, I felt that the glory of the hoped-for prophecies would more than make up for them. I remember well how I used to hang about any "traveling Friends" who might come to the house, in the hope that at some unexpected moment the Divine afflatus would come upon them, and the "message" I longed for might be delivered to me.

For it must be understood that these "Opportunities" were never by any manner of means arranged for. They were always ushered in by a solemn hush falling suddenly upon the company, and this hush might come at any moment, even the most inconvenient; but, wherever it was or whatever was going on, everything had to give way for it. I have known "Opportunities" to come in the middle of a social evening, or even in the midst of a meal, or when the preacher was bidding farewell to the household, or when taking a walk with some one, or when going to bed in the same room with a friend. They often came most inconveniently; but nothing was allowed to hinder. I remember once assisting at one when I was waiting on a preaching aunt on a visit to a Friend's house in Burlington, New Jersey. We had packed our trunks, and they were piled on the carriage at the door ready to take us to the train, when suddenly, as we were standing up bidding our hosts farewell, a silence fell, and an "Opportunity" came upon my aunt, and, while I stood, holding her shawl, in a fever of impatience to be gone, she had to stop and deliver her message, regardless of all considerations of time and trains. I was a woman by this time, and had lost a little of my faith in the divine origin of these "Opportunities," and I remember that I could not help upbraiding her a little, when at last we got off to our train, for the inopportune moment she had chosen. But her reply silenced me when she said with the most guileless faith, "But, my dear, I could not disobey my Guide, and thee sees He has brought us to the train in time after all."

No one but those who had experienced them could possibly understand the profound impression these "Opportunities" made upon the Quaker life of my childhood. And even to this day when, as sometimes happens, a silence for a moment suddenly falls upon a company, my first instinctive terror is lest it should be an "opportunity," and somebody should have to preach.

The awe-inspiring effect of these "opportunities," and the absolute confidence that was placed in the messages so delivered, cannot be better illustrated than by what happened during a visit of some "English Friends" to our meetings in Philadelphia, when I was about seventeen. I should say here that it was the custom among the "Friends" for preachers in different places to have what they called "religious concerns" to visit other Meetings and neighborhoods, in, as they quaintly expressed it, "the service of Truth." These visits were always occasions of great interest to us young people, even though the preacher might not have come from any great distance; but when they came from England, which was to us an unknown land of grandeur and of mystery, our awe and reverence knew no bounds. "English Friends" seemed to us almost like visitants from an angelic sphere; and to be noticed or spoken to by one of them made the fortunate recipients feel as though Heaven itself had come down to them.

The English Friends I speak of were entertained, during their stay in Philadelphia, by Marmaduke and Sarah Cope, who lived in Filbert Street opposite to our house. Their daughter Madgie, was an intimate friend of mine, and one morning she came to me in a great state of excitement over a remarkable "Opportunity," which she said one of the "English Friends" had had the evening before with a young man we both knew. She said some Friends had dropped in to see the English Friends, and during the course of the evening, an "Opportunity" had come upon them, and one of the traveling Friends had begun to preach. After a short exhortation, he had sin-

gled out this young man, and had addressed him in a most remarkable manner, telling him that he had received a direct call from God
to enter into the ministry, and prophesying that he was to become a
great preacher, and was to visit far distant lands in the "service of
Truth."

I can remember vividly to this day the profound impression made
upon me by this occurrence. The preacher who had delivered the
message to this young man was one upon whom I had placed all my
hopes for a direct message, and had been disappointed; and now he
had prophesied about a young man, who in my opinion was no
more deserving than myself, the very things that I was always wanting some preacher to prophesy about me. I confess I felt deep pangs
of jealousy that the "Divine favor" should have overlooked me,
and been bestowed upon one who really seemed to me no more
worthy. However, it was all a part of the great romance of our lives,
and there was always the possibility that it might still, at some
blessed "Opportunity," be bestowed upon me, and I went about for
days full of the subject.

A day or two after it occurred I was out driving with a very especial friend, the one who, as will appear in another part of my
story, had been the means of my awakening at sixteen. I was at this
time nearly seventeen, and my friend was perhaps nine or ten years
older. I had for her a very adoring friendship, and always poured
out into her sympathizing ears everything that interested me. Being
this day full of the subject, I of course detailed the whole story to
her, investing it with all the importance it had assumed in my own
eyes. My friend seemed deeply interested, and asked a great many
questions as to the details of the "message" and how it had affected
the young man. Not many weeks afterwards she told me she was
engaged to be married to this very young man, and confessed that
she had been largely influenced in her decision by what I had told
her, as she was sure the prophecy made in that "Opportunity"
would be fulfilled, and she felt it would be a great privilege to be
united to one whose future was to be so full of work in the "service
of Truth."

I have always watched the career of that young man with the
deepest interest, because I could not help feeling at the time that he
had received a message which by rights ought to have come to me;
and I must confess that the prophecies which made me so jealous
have never been fulfilled in his case; and, now that we are both old
people, I cannot but see that my life has come far nearer their ful-

fillment than his. He has been a most upright, conscientious man, and truly religious in a quiet way, but he has never become a preacher, nor done any public Christian work. While I without any "message" or any "call," such as I was always longing for, and supposed to be necessary, did become a preacher and have tried to proclaim in many countries the "good news of the gospel of the Lord Jesus Christ."

In this case, therefore, the "message" seemed to fail to find entrance. But on so many occasions similar messages were so marvelously fulfilled, and the accounts of these cases were so constantly retailed to us as strengtheners to our faith, that it is no wonder we grew up with a profound belief in their infallibility. I have many times known a Quaker preacher in a "Meeting" or an "Opportunity" make a revelation to an individual present of something known only to that individual, or prophesy something for the future of an individual or of a community, of which there was no present indication, but which came true just as it had been declared it would.

I knew one woman Friend, who seemed to have this gift in a remarkable degree. I remember her once stopping in the middle of a sermon she was preaching at a week-day meeting to a congregation of entire strangers, and saying, "A young man has entered this room who has in his pocket some papers by means of which he is about to commit a great sin. If he will come to see me this afternoon at ——— (mentioning the house at which she was staying), I have a message from the Lord to give him that will show him a way out of his trouble." She then resumed her sermon where she had left off, and said nothing further of the incident. I was very much interested to follow this up, and I found a strange young man did in fact call on the preacher that afternoon and confess that he had a forged check in his pocket, which he was on his way to cash, when some influence, he could not tell what, had induced him to turn into the Meeting-house as he was passing. His name was not asked for nor given, but the message from the Lord was delivered, and the young man tore up the forged check in the preacher's presence, and promised to lead a new life. And some years afterwards the preacher met him and found that this promise had been fulfilled.

On another occasion, when this same preacher was staying in the country at the house of a cousin of mine, she came down to breakfast one morning and said that the Lord had revealed to her in the night that she was to take a message to a man living some miles off.

No name had been given her, nor any indication as to the where-abouts of the man she was to see, but she told my cousin, that, if he would take her in his carriage, she was sure the Lord would show them in which direction to go. They set out therefore, and the preacher pointed out one road after another which they were to take, and, finally, when about six miles from home, and in a part of the country about which neither the preacher nor my cousin knew anything, she pointed to a house they saw in the distance, and said, "That is the house, and when we get there I shall find one man in the garden, and thou may wait for me at the gate." They accordingly stopped at this house, and, while my cousin waited, the preacher went straight through the grounds into the garden, and delivered her message to the man she found there. She told him he was contemplating a very wrong action which would bring great trouble upon himself and his family, but the Lord was willing to deliver him, and had sent her to open his eyes to the sin and the danger of what he had decided to do. The man was deeply impressed, and, after a little hesitation, confessed that all she had said was true, and that that very day had been the time when his plan was to have been carried out, but that now he dared not go on with it. He then and there gave it up, and said, after such a manifest token of God's interest in him, he would put the whole matter into His care, and would trust Him to manage it. And after events proved that this had been really done, and that all had turned out far better than he could have expected.

Were there space I could relate hundreds of similar incidents, but these will suffice. It will easily be understood, however, that, in the face of facts such as these, it is not to be wondered at that we were full of faith. Until I was married, a Minister was to me a person altogether removed from the ordinary ranks of men and women, a being almost from another sphere, with none of the common weaknesses of humanity, set apart for a Divine work, and endowed with almost Divine attributes. When I was a child I used to sit and watch them in "meeting" as they sat in long rows on the high benches facing the audience, the men on one side and the women on the other, expecting every minute to see revealed the halo which I was sure must be encircling their heads, although invisible to me. And sometimes, when I got tired of waiting, I would screw up my eyes until I created a sort of shining circle around every object I looked at, and then tried to persuade myself that this was the invisible halo I was so longing to see.

As I grew older these fancies of course left me; but for many years a delightful mystery and awe still encircled the "gallery Friends": and the coming of a "traveling Minister" continued to fill me with eager and delicious expectations. Especially was this the case after my awakening at sixteen. In my diary I wrote in reference to the very Minister who had given that wonderful message to the young man, as follows:—

"11/29/1848. I heard to-day the most delightful news I have heard for a long time. The English Friends, *dear* Benjamin Seebohm and Robert Lindsay, are expected in town by next First Day. Oh! won't it be joyful! joyful! They will be at our First Day evening meeting. Hurrah! Oh! I am so glad I can hardly contain myself. I am very different from what I was when they were here last.

> Deeper than the gilded surface
>   Hath my wakeful vision seen,
> Further than the narrow present
>   Have my journeyings been.
> I have, midst life's empty visions,
>   Heard the solemn step of time,
> And the low mysterious voices
>   Of another clime.
> All the mystery of Being
>   Has upon my Spirit pressed;
> Thoughts which, like the Deluge wanderer
>   Find no place of rest."

I fully expected these inspired Friends to know by inward revelation all I had been going through, and of course hoped they would have a Divine message for me, direct from God. The longed for First Day came and I went to meeting with my brother, full of fearsome yet delicious anticipations. But alas! as was always the case with me, I was doomed to disappointment. Still it might come another time, and I lived in hope.

It was this constant expectation of a direct word from God that made the romance of my young life, and that was I feel sure, one of the secrets of the great hold Quakerism had on the young people of my day.

But, except for this inspirational preaching, we received from our society very little definite religious teaching of any kind. We had, as I have said, no Sunday-schools, and no Bible classes, and doctrines and dogmas were, to me at least, an absolutely unknown quantity. We had no Catechism and were not even taught the Ten Commandments, as they were felt to belong to the old Jewish dispensation which had passed away in Christ. I do not suppose that I was ever told so, but I had a distinct feeling as a child that the Ten Commandments, like the Lord's Prayer, were for "worldly" uses. I felt somehow that they belonged only to the outside world (*i.e.*, all who were not Friends), who probably needed outward commandments to keep them good, while we Friends were to be good from deeper motives. For it was not that the moral training of the "Ten Commandments" had ceased to be binding, but that the Friends believed it was far more fully taught in the new commandments of the dispensation of Christ, which were to be written, not on tables of stone, nor even on the pages of a book, but upon the spiritual tablets of our hearts.

They believed that, because we were in Christ, we were to be controlled by a law from within and not by a law from without; and to them it was literally true that for people who were led of the Spirit, there "was no law." They taught that the fruit of the indwelling Spirit would necessarily be the fulfilling of the law, and that therefore no outward law would be needed; that, just as a man who is honest at heart needs no law to keep him from dishonesty, so, if a man is truly a Christian, he will need no law to make him act as a Christian ought to act. He will do it by the impulse of his inward life. The early Friends fully believed that if God has possession of the heart He will work in us both to will and to do of His own good pleasure, and that an outward law, therefore, would be a superfluity. We were consequently directed to yield ourselves to this inward Divine working, and to listen for the Voice of the Holy Spirit in our hearts; and we were taught that, when this Voice was heard, it must be implicitly and faithfully obeyed.

We were to expect to hear this "inward voice" at any or all times, and about all things; but were encouraged to look for it especially in our "meetings for worship" when the whole congregation were sitting in silence "before the Lord." Quaker meetings were always held on this basis of silent waiting, in order that in the silence the Holy Spirit might have an opportunity of speaking directly to each individual soul. The Friends recognized the unseen but living presence of Christ in their meetings, and no individual was set apart to "conduct their service," or to be a mediator between their souls and their invisible Teacher. The silence might not be broken by any one, not even by an "acknowledged Minister," except under a sense of the direct and immediate guidance of the Spirit; but, under that guidance, any one, even the poorest washer-woman or the smallest child, might deliver the "message." This gave a mysterious and even romantic interest to our meetings, as we never knew what might happen, or who, even perhaps ourselves, might be "led" to take part.

I cannot say, however, that anything especial ever came to me in any meeting. Now and then a sermon would be preached that seemed perhaps to apply to my case, but never strikingly enough to really impress me; and now and then it would happen that by some mysterious influence my heart would be "tendered," as it was termed, and I would feel for a little while as though God did after all care for me and would help me. But as a general thing my "meetings" were mostly passed in building air castles, an occupation that I felt to be very wrong, but which had an irresistible fascination for me. Curiously enough, these day dreams never took the form of love stories, as youthful air castles so generally do, I suppose because I had never been allowed to read novels, and never heard anything about falling in love. But I always made myself out to be something very wonderful and grand, and the admired of all beholders. Sometimes I was to be a preacher whose eloquence was to surpass the eloquence of all preachers since the world began; sometimes I was to be an inventor of more wonderful machines than ever had been invented before; but more often I was to be the most marvelous singer the world had ever known; and the "meetings" that stand out in my memory more distinctly than any other, were those of one especial winter in my fourteenth year, when I endowed myself with an undreamed of gift for singing, that electrified everybody, and brought the world to my feet. Why I pitched on singing for my day dreams I cannot imagine, as it was a forbidden worldliness among the Quakers, and was something I scarcely ever heard, either in public or private; and I was myself so utterly devoid of any musical talent that during my whole life I have not been able to sing a note, or even to distinguish one tune from another. But so it was; and there I used to sit on the bench beside my mother, through many a long meeting, outwardly a demure little Quaker, but inwardly a great prima donna, (not that I called myself that) with my whole foolish little heart swelling and bursting with the glory of my triumphs on the stage, which however was a place I had never even so much as seen!

Sometimes, however, my conscience would not permit me to indulge in my day dreams, and then my "meetings" would be filled with futile struggles against wandering thoughts, or with vain efforts to resist an uncontrollable desire to sleep, for to "sleep in meeting" was felt by all of us to be almost a crowning disgrace.

Whether on the whole those long, solemn meetings, with their great stretches of silence, and with sermons, when there were any, that made very little direct appeal to me, were or were not a valuable part of my religious training. I do not feel prepared to say. But one thing is certain, that, whether from the preaching in our meetings, or from the conversation of our elders, or from the atmosphere around us, there were certain strong impressions made upon me which stand out vividly in my memory.

CHAPTER SIX

QUAKER GUIDANCE

*T*he strongest impression made upon my young heart was the paramount privilege we as Quakers enjoyed in our knowledge of the "perceptible guidance" of the Holy Spirit, and the vital necessity of obedience to this guidance. It was fully believed by us young Friends that our "Society" was the sole depository of this knowledge; and although it was for the most part a great mystery to us, yet still we could not help feeling a certain pride in such a distinctive possession. That it was regarded by the Friends as a very real thing, was proved by the fact that anything which professed to be the result of this guidance was treated with the most profound respect and consideration. If even a child could say it felt a Divine "leading" in any direction, that leading was treated with loving consideration by the older Friends, and, unless it was manifestly improper, way was tenderly made for it to be carried out. For Friends believed their children were every one included among the lambs of the flock, and had the same privileges of hearing the voice of the Good Shepherd that their parents possessed.

A very striking illustration of this reverence for anything that was felt to be from Divine guidance occurred two hundred years ago in our own family history, An aunt of one of our great-grandfathers was a certain Elizabeth Haddon, who was the daughter of a wealthy Friend named John Haddon, living in Rotherhithe, now a suburb of London. John Haddon had purchased some land in New Jersey, intending to remove there with his family, and had even sent out mechanics who had built a suitable house and outbuildings. But meantime circumstances had made it necessary for him to remain in England. His young daughter Elizabeth, just eighteen, who believed she had felt a call to work in New Jersey, was greatly disappointed, but, as she prayed about it, she seemed to hear an inward voice telling her that she must take up the family burden and go over herself to the New World and develop the property there. She called her family together and told them of her impressions of duty. She was very young, and the country was unsettled, and her parents were frightened. But they were staunch Quakers, and they had always taught their children an implicit obedience to what the voice of the Lord might require, and they did not dare to oppose what their young daughter felt so strongly to be her duty, and, although in much fear and trembling, they made arrangements for her emigration.

This was in 1701. She found the country in a very rough state, but lived there long enough to see the whole neighborhood, largely through her own instrumentality, revolutionized into a most prosperous community, to which she was for many years an untold blessing. The town that sprang up near her home was called Haddonfield after her, and for many years our father had a country house not far off, where we entered into the fruits of our great-aunt's labors.

An American historian in relating her story says:

"Among the many singular manifestations of strong faith and religious zeal, connected with the settlement of this country, few are more remarkable than the voluntary separation of this girl of eighteen from a wealthy home and all the associations of childhood, to go to a distant and unsettled country to fulfill what she considered a religious duty; and the humble self-sacrificing faith of the parents in giving up their beloved child with such reverent tenderness for the promptings of her own conscience, has in it something sublimely beautiful, if we look at it in its own pure light."

This absolute independence in all matters of felt duty has always seemed to me to be one of our greatest Quaker privileges. It left every individual free to serve God in the way that seemed right, without the often kindly meant but hindering interference of those around them. To say simply, "I feel it right to do so and so," invariably silenced all objections.

Nor was this only the case in spiritual matters, but in earthly matters as well, and it gave to each individual that position of independence which has always to my mind seemed one of the most vital of human needs. And I look upon the sense of personal ownership engendered by all this, as one of the most priceless of all the gifts that my Quaker inheritance has brought me.

I remember when I first waked up to the injustices of the position of women in the outside world, I was able to congratulate myself continually that it was so much better among "Friends"; and that not the most tyrannical "man Friend," even if he wanted to, would ever dare to curtail the liberty of his womenkind, if only they could say they "felt a concern" for any course of action.

To interfere between any soul and its Divine Guide, except under a Divine constraint, was considered by the Friends to be one of the gravest wrongs that one person could inflict upon another; and in all my experience of Quakerism in my young days I have no recollection of its ever having been done, except by the Elders and Overseers. A Quaker "concern" was to my mind clothed with even more authority than the Bible, for the Bible was God's voice of long ago, while the "concern" was His voice at the present moment, and, as such, was of far greater present importance. I do not suppose any one ever taught me definitely that this was the case, but the whole atmosphere around me, and the preaching I heard, was certainly calculated to exalt the "inward voice" and its communications above all other voices, and to make us feel that since God spoke to us directly, we need not search into what He might say to any one outside of our sacred fold.

It might naturally be thought that this liberty in individual guidance would have led into extravagances, and in the early days of the society this sometimes happened. But in my time the Friends safeguarded their members from this danger by requiring all "concerns" or "leadings" that were at all out of the ordinary, to be brought before the Elders and Overseers, and judged by them in a solemn season of waiting upon God for His teaching. And, so convinced were all Friends that the collective voice of the Holy Spirit in a meeting was of more authority than a private voice to an individual, that decisions arrived at under such circumstances were always accepted as final, and the conscience of the individual, whose "leading" was set aside, felt itself freed from the burden. It was an admirable safeguard, and during all my years of close association with the society I never knew of any instance of serious extravagance.

Apart from this teaching of the perceptible guidance of the Holy Spirit, nothing very definite or tangible was taught us. As far as I can remember we were never told we had to be "converted" or "born again," and my own impression was that these were things, which might be necessary for the "world's people," but were entirely unnecessary for us, who were birthright members of the Society of Friends, and were already born into the kingdom of God, and only needed to be exhorted to live up to our high calling. I believe this was because of one of the fundamental principles of Quakerism, which was a belief in the universal fatherhood of God, and a recognition of the fact that Christ had linked Himself on to humanity, and had embraced the whole world in His divine brotherhood, so that every soul that was born belonged to Him, and could claim sonship with the same Father. "My Father and your Father," He says, and the early Friends accepted this as true, and would have thought it misleading therefore to urge us to become what we already were. We were always preached to as "lambs of the flock," and as only needing to be obedient to the voice of the Good Shepherd, to whom we already belonged. The Friends did not shut their children out, but instead, with loving tenderness, shut them inside the heavenly fold; and all their teaching was to this effect.

For a little time, in my Plymouth brethren days, I looked upon this as a dreadful heresy; but later on I learned the blessed fact, stated by Paul to the heathen idolaters at Athens, that we are all, the heathen even included, "God's offspring"; and I realized that, since He is our creator, He is of course our Father, and we equally of course are His children. And I learned to thank and bless the grand old Quakers who had made this discovery, since their teaching made it easy for me to throw aside the limiting, narrowing ideas I had at first adopted, and helped me to comprehend the glorious fact that in God we all "live and move and have our being," and that therefore no one can shut another out.

CHAPTER SEVEN

QUAKER QUERIES

*N*ext in importance to the impression made upon my young mind by this teaching regarding the perceptible guidance of the Holy Spirit, was the one made by "Friends' testimonies," as they were called, and the "Queries" that were founded upon them. These "Queries" were a series of questions in regard to the practice of Quakerism, which were solemnly asked and answered once a month in Monthly Meetings, appointed for the purpose of transacting the business of the society. There were eight of these "Queries," and they contained a splendid code of morals, calculated to develop a people of unflinching uprightness and honesty in all their dealings with their fellowmen, and of a grand self-restraint and self-denial in their private lives; and, much as I chafed at them as a child, I have never been able to forget the lessons they taught, and often to this day find myself guided by their precepts.

With such a monthly probing of conduct as these Queries compelled, it was almost a necessity that a high standard of righteousness should have become an integral part of a Quaker's life; and I feel it to have been an invaluable element of my own religious training.

Back of these Queries there was a body of "Friends' testimonies" from which the Queries had arisen, which although unwritten, except so far as they were expressed in the Queries, were absolutely binding upon every true Friend. I have often thought that they were in reality, though no one said so, our Quaker Ten Commandments, which we had put in the place of the Jewish ones. I certainly believed as a child that they were in fact the especial commandments that had been given to us as Quakers, which differentiated us from all the Christians around us, and made us the "peculiar people" we were proud to call ourselves. They were many of them very strict and severe, and to an outsider must often have seemed rather painful; but, as all the Quakers I knew had been brought up on them from infancy, they did not press as heavily upon us as might have been supposed. But they certainly did serve to keep Quaker feet walking in a narrow way, which way we believed to be the actual "strait gate and narrow way" spoken of in the Bible as the only path that "leadeth unto life." Every one of these "testimonies" had been, we were devoutly convinced, directly revealed by the Holy Spirit to the "early Friends"; and consequently, however unreasonable they might otherwise have seemed to us, we young Friends in my day reverenced them as the very oracles of God.

As these Queries seem to have almost entirely fallen into the background among the Quakers of late years, I will record them here, as a true exposition of the Quakerism of my young days.

"*First Query.* —Are all our religious meetings for worship and discipline duly attended; is the hour observed; and are Friends clear of sleeping, and of all other unbecoming behavior therein?

"*Second Query.* —Are love and unity maintained amongst you? Are tale-bearing and detraction discouraged? And where any differences arise, are endeavors used speedily to end them?

"*Third Query.* —Are Friends careful to bring up those under their direction, in plainness of speech, behavior and apparel; in frequently reading the Holy Scriptures, and to restrain them from reading pernicious books, and from the corrupt conversation of the world? And are they good examples in these respects themselves?

"*Fourth Query.* —Are Friends careful to discourage the unnecessary distillation and use of spirituous liquors, and the frequenting of taverns; to avoid places of diversion; and to keep in true moderation and temperance on the account of marriages, burials and all other occasions?

"*Fifth Query.* —Are poor Friends' necessities duly inspected, and they relieved or assisted in such business as they are capable of? Do their children freely partake of learning to fit them for business; and are they and other Friends' children placed among Friends?

"*Sixth Query.* —Do you maintain a faithful testimony against oaths; an hireling ministry; bearing arms, training, and other military services; being concerned in any fraudulent or clandestine trade; buying or vending goods so imported; or prize goods; and against encouraging lotteries of any kind?

"*Seventh Query.* —Are Friends careful to live within the bounds of their circumstances, and to keep to moderation in their trade or business? Are they punctual to their promises, and just in the payment of their debts; and are such as give reasonable grounds for fear on these accounts, timely labored with for their preservation or recovery?

"*Eighth Query.* —Do you take due care regularly to deal with all offenders in the spirit of meekness, without partiality or unnecessary delay, in order for their help; and where such labor is ineffectual, to place judgment upon them, in the authority of truth?"

The reading of these Queries in our Monthly Meetings constituted a sort of monthly confessional for the whole society, and were seasons of solemn self-examination for both old and young. Each separate Meeting belonging to the "Monthly Meeting" sent in its own set of answers for this public confessional, and the consideration of these answers was called the "consideration of the state of society."

"Our meetings have all been duly attended by most of our members, but some Friends have not observed the hour."—"Mostly clear of unbecoming behavior, but some sleeping has been observed."—"Friends generally are careful to bring up their children in plainness of speech, behavior, and apparel, but more faithfulness in this respect is desirable."—"Our testimony against oaths and a hireling ministry, bearing arms, being concerned in any clandestine trade, and against encouraging lotteries, has been faithfully maintained by all our members." Such were some of the answers that linger in my memory.

It was the custom after each Query and answer had been read, for a time of silence to be observed in order to give Friends an opportunity to "relieve their minds" of any message that might have been given them concerning that especial Query; and these opportunities were generally times of great searchings of heart with all who were present.

As I remember it, the one Query that was preached about the most frequently and the most fervently was the Third, concerning the testimony for "plainness of speech, behavior, and apparel, and against the vain fashions of the world." It was this testimony that did the most to make Quakers a "peculiar people," and that caused us young Quakers the worst of our heart burnings. I remember to this day the sufferings I used to undergo each month as I sat beside my mother and heard this Query read and preached about. My constant fear was lest it should make her more strict in trying to keep us from the "vain fashions of the world," which, in spite of our training, possessed a fascination we could not wholly conquer. As the Friend who was appointed to read the Queries approached this especial one, I used to do my best to abstract my mind, and would even surreptitiously stop my ears, trying to cheat myself into thinking that, if I did not notice it, my mother would not either. But alas! as I recall those days, I must acknowledge that I was always doomed to disappointment, for, as I have said, the preaching about this particular Query was the most frequent and the most fervent, and in the end I, as well as my mother was always obliged to listen.

Two incidents of my childhood, connected with this Query, come up very vividly before me.

Our mother had bought us some white china crepe shawls with lovely long fringes that seemed to us too beautiful for words, and we wore them with the greatest pride. But one day she came home from a meeting where the Queries had been read and answered, and told us she had felt in meeting that our long fringes were too "worldly" for "Friends' children," and she believed it was her duty to cut them shorter. I can see it all to-day, as she carefully spread the shawls out on a large table, and laid a yardstick along the fringe at what she considered was the right length, and proceeded to cut off all the lovely beautiful extra lengths. It was like cutting into our very vitals, and I remember well how we pleaded and pleaded that the fatal yardstick might be slipped down just a little further. Our great fear was that our fringes would be cut shorter than the fringes of similar shawls that had been purchased at the same time for our most intimate friends, Hannah and Jane Scull, who were a little gayer than ourselves. To have their fringes, even so much as the tenth of an inch longer than ours, seemed to us a catastrophe not to be borne. I do not remember how it turned out in the end, but I shall never forget to my dying day the agonies of mind we went through in the process.

Another experience about dress left an indelible impression on my mind. The shape of sleeve that was considered "plain" in my day was what are called leg-of-mutton sleeves, and the sleeves of all our dresses were of this orthodox leg-of-mutton shape. But some benign influence, what it was we never understood, induced our mother one spring to let us have our sleeves made a little in the fashion, which happened at that time to be what was called Bishop sleeves, full at both the shoulder and the wrist. The fashion was for very large and full "Bishops" and ours were tiny little ones, but they were real "Bishops" and our pride in them was immense. The dresses were our new spring school dresses, of a brown and white striped print, calico, we called it. They were finished while the weather was still very wintry-like, but so great was our desire to show off our fashionable sleeves to the astonished world, that nothing would do but we must put them on and go for a long walk without any coats; and no two prouder little girls were abroad in the whole world that morning than Hannah and Sally Whitall, as they walked along the streets of Philadelphia in their fashionable attire. I remember our younger sister Mary wanted to go with us, but her sleeves were still leg-of-mutton, and we felt it would take from the full effect, if one member of our party should display the despised sleeves, and we made her walk on the opposite side of the way. I can see her longing glances across the street now, as she admired our glory from afar. However, she had her revenge not long after, for ruffled panties (as we called drawers then) coming down to the feet, had come into fashion, and as our mother was making her a new set, they were made long and ruffled, while we still had to wear our plain hemmed ones, not showing below our dresses. And

81

this time she also went out to walk to show her new panties, but, kinder than we had been, she invited us to accompany her. I am sorry to say, however, that the old Adam in us resented her favored condition so strongly, that we refused to walk on the same side of the street with her, and scornfully crossed over to the other side, leaving her to walk alone, with all the glory taken out of her beautiful ruffled "panties" by our cruel scorn and unkindness.

The early Friends, in order to testify against the foolish changes of fashion among the "world's people" had, as far as possible, adhered to the style of dress that was being worn when they took their rise, and in a very few years this naturally grew peculiar, and finally became a sort of Quaker uniform, which all good Friends felt "led" to adopt. I say they adhered to the first style as far as possible, because moderate changes were inevitable from the fact that certain styles, when they ceased to be fashionable, dropped sooner or later out of the market, and could no longer be easily procured; and also because the views, even the strictest, could not help being more or less modified by time and use.

The fact was that their "testimony" as to "plainness of apparel" was not a testimony against or for any special style of dress, but it was simply a testimony against following the "vain fashions of the world"; and by the time a style had become old-fashioned, and was going out, the Quakers would be prepared to adopt it.

I met lately in some extracts from an old diary the following curious illustration of this. In the time of Queen Elizabeth, before Quakers arose, it was the general fashion to wear green aprons as a part of a lady's church-going dress; but by the time the Quakers came on the scene this fashion had begun to die out, and starched white aprons were taking the place of green in the fashionable world. In order not to follow the changing fashions, Friends held on to the green aprons for their go-to-meeting dress, and their preachers preached against the fashionable white aprons as being of a "gay and polluting color." One old preacher, it is recorded, declared in one of his sermons, that the starch water used to stiffen these aprons was the "devil's water with which they needed to be sprinkled," and warned his hearers against its polluting use.

Curiously enough, this rooted Quaker objection to following the vain fashions of the world extended even to many useful inventions of which one would have supposed the practical good sense of the Friends would have seen the value. I remember that when sewing machines first came into vogue they were considered by the Friends exceedingly worldly. And, when I had made up my mind to buy one, I was obliged to make my purchase in secret, and to hide the machine in the most inaccessible room in my house, in order that no one might be grieved with my worldliness. Of course later on, when the Friends had got used to the innovation, sewing machines were to be seen in every well-ordered Quaker household; but for a long time I went about with a haunting sense of having fallen from grace, because of the worldly thing I had purchased.

The standard of plainness, therefore, necessarily varied from one generation to another. But whatever the standard might be, the "testimony" against the vain fashions of the world continued the same, and each generation felt that the established costume of their day was of the nature of a Divine ordinance, especially patterned in Heaven itself.

This conviction of the sanctity of the "plain dress" arose largely, I believe, from the fact that all their own personal religion had come to them through this channel. The newly awakened Friend, whether young or old, was invariably confronted with the question of "becoming plain"; and the surrender of will involved in giving up to adopt the Quaker uniform always brought such peace and rest of soul, that it was almost inevitable they should consider the putting on of the "plain dress" as being the procuring cause of the blessing. This was especially the case with our own dear father. In his diary, under date of 1823 when he was just twenty-three years old, he writes:

"While at home from my fifth voyage I believed it right to adopt the plain dress and language of Friends. While under the conviction of its being right, and fearing I should lose my situation if I did so, I met with Samuel Bettle, Sr., who, without knowing the distressed state of my mind, told me, if I was faithful to what I felt to be right, the Lord would make a way for me where there seemed no way; which indeed He did, giving me favour in the sight of my employer much to my comfort. Hearing of a ship as needing a chief mate, I borrowed a plain coat of my friend, James Cox, my own not being ready, and called to see the captain, telling him I could not "Mr." and "Sir" him as was common. To which he replied kindly that it would only be a nine days' wonder, and at once engaged me as first mate. Thus my prayer was answered and a way made for me where I saw no way. Praised forever be the name of the Lord."

This was the turning point in his religious life, and it was followed by such an uplifting of soul, and such a sense of the love of God, that he was never able to dissociate them, and all his life believed, that, if any one else would adopt the same dress, the same blessing would follow. I believe he would freely have bestowed a "plain coat" as a gift upon anybody who would wear one; and nothing ever seemed to disturb his profound conviction that "plain coats" and "plain bonnets" had been shaped and patterned in Heaven. He even assured us once that he fully believed that the armies in Heaven, spoken of in Rev. 19:14, who followed the King of kings on white horses, all had on "plain coats"! He was a member of the Board of a Quaker college near Philadelphia, which required all its students to wear the "plain" straight-collared coats. But in hot summer weather, when the students were obliged to wear linen or seersucker coats on account of the heat, their thin straight collars refused to stand up, and wilted down with the heat. The question came before the Board as to whether, under such circumstances, they might not be allowed to wear turned-down collars. Some of the Board were for yielding, but our dear father would not listen to this for a moment, but declared that, if there were no other way of making their collars stand, they must put whalebone in to stiffen them, for "stand they must." I believe however that the summer heats were too much for even his stalwart principles, and he was at last forced reluctantly to consent to the turned over collars.

I have no doubt the same thing occurs in other denominations besides Friends. They have their own especial forms and ceremonies, which are more or less incumbent upon their members, submission to which very often results in blessings of peace and rest of soul similar to those the Friends experienced when putting on the "plain dress"; and, like the Friends, many of them have no doubt supposed these forms or ceremonies to be the procuring cause of the blessings, and have in consequence exalted them into a place of sanctity, and have even believed them to have been ordained and patterned in heaven. I realized this very strongly not long ago when attending a Roman Catholic Mass in Italy. I was inclined to be critical over the gorgeous robes of the priests, saying to myself that the Lord could not possibly care for such things, when it flashed into my mind that after all there was no radical difference between a robe of crimson and gold, and a black coat with a straight collar, or between a Sister of Charity's quaint costume, and a sugar-scoop bonnet and a dove-colored shawl; and I saw that just as the Quakers of my childhood had been sure that their "plain" clothes were pleasing to God, so also these devoted priests were sure that their gorgeous robes were acceptable in the Divine sight. Each party believed they were obeying the Lord in regard to their dress, and their obedience to what they believed to be right was after all the essential point.

I have had no difficulty since then in feeling absolute Christian charity towards every honest form of ceremony, let it be as contrary to my own ideas as it may, for I realize that it is true that "the Lord seeth not as man seeth; for man looketh on the outward appearance, but the Lord looketh on the heart."

CHAPTER EIGHT

THE "SUGAR-SCOOP" BONNET

*O*ne of the most prominent features of the "plainness of apparel" of my day was the bonnet worn by all good women Friends, which, from its shape, we young people irreverently called a "sugar-scoop," although it often seemed, to me at least, that we committed a sacrilege in daring to treat the sacred bonnet in such a fashion. For that it was sacred no young Quaker of my day would have dreamed of denying. A late writer, dealing with a little later date than my own, says concerning it:

> "To one brought up 'within the fold' it is no light matter to approach so awful a subject as the Quaker bonnet. There was a solemnity about it that was born of terror. Whether it presided at the head of the 'women's meeting' or ventured in winter storms, protected in its satin or oilskin case under the Friendly umbrella, or even lay alone in splendid state upon the bed of the welcome guest; anywhere, everywhere, it was a solemn thing."[1]

[1]"The Evolution of the Quaker Dress," by A. S. Grummere.

Why this bonnet which was always made of a very delicate light silk, and was exceedingly expensive and difficult to make, and most uncomfortable to wear, should have been considered "plain," while a simple straw bonnet without trimming which would cost only a quarter as much, and would be infinitely more comfortable, should be considered "gay," is a mystery. But so it was, and whenever a "plain bonnet" was spoken of, only a "sugar-scoop" was ever meant.

The other articles of a woman Friend's "plain dress" in my day were a silk shawl of a soft dove color folded over a plain-waisted, low-necked, dove-colored or brown dress, with folds of thin white muslin filling up the neck and crossed over the bosom, and a thin muslin cap of the same shape as the bonnet, tied under the chin with soft white ribbons, and always worn both indoors, and out under the "sugar-scoop." In cold weather they had large dove-colored cashmere shawls for outdoors, or cashmere Mother Hubbard cloaks pleated on to a yoke, with a silk-lined hood. These shawls were always folded with a point down the middle of the back, and with three accurate folds at the neck immediately over this point, held by a stout pin. There was also a pin on each shoulder to hold the full-ness steady, skillfully hidden to make it look as though the fullness held itself, and the shawl fell gracefully apart in front to reveal the crossed handkerchief of tulle or thin muslin that was crossed over the Quakerly bosom.

The "plain clothes" for the men were a cut-away coat with a straight clergyman's collar, and a broad-brimmed hat. The whole costume was very quaint, and, for the women Friends, very becom-ing, and I do not think I have ever seen sweeter faces anywhere than the placid, gentle faces inside these caps and bonnets; and I cannot but feel that the world is poorer for the disappearance of these quaint old costumes.

As a consequence of the fact that all Quakers both young and old were, as I have shown, treated as though they were "in the fold," and were therefore never exhorted to become converted in order to get in, the only thing we knew about, as indicating a change in any one's religious experience, was what was called "becoming seri-ous" or "becoming plain," and this was always expressed out-wardly by the adoption of the "plain dress" of the society.

The putting on of this "plain dress" was looked forward to by us young people as an inevitable fate that awaited all Quaker children, but a fate that was to be deferred by every known device as long as possible. The usual time for its happening in Philadelphia where I lived, was at the spring "Yearly Meeting," which occurred in April, and at which time we all came out in our new spring clothes. It was then that the fate was most likely to descend upon its victims, and the young men and women of the society, who had "become serious," would feel it their duty to appear at "Yearly Meeting" in the sugar-scoop bonnets, or the straight-collared coats and broad-brimmed hats, that were the outward badge of their inward change. I remember well how those of us upon whom the fate had not yet fallen, used to go to the first meeting of the "Yearly Meeting" early, and sit on benches where we could keep a good outlook on every one who came in, and watch to see which one of our friends and comrades had been snatched from our ranks to wear these distinguishing badges of having "become serious." Of all the wrestlings and agonizing that preceded this open confession of a change of heart we were only dimly aware, but there was enough solemnity and strangeness about the whole thing to make us feel that henceforth our comrades belonged to another world from ours. And when, as often happened, this adopting of the peculiar Quaker garb was also accompanied by a few words spoken tremblingly in some Meeting by the young neophyte, we felt that the gulf between us could never be crossed until we too became the victims of a similar fate.

No words I could use could fully express the awful solemnity that, to my young mind at least, invested this fate. To "put on a plain bonnet," as it was expressed, seemed to me almost as much the end of all earthly human life as death would be. After it, one could never again live as other people did. If one was young, one could never have any more fun, for it was evident that races could not be run, nor trees climbed, nor haymows scaled, in a dove-colored "sugar-scoop bonnet." If one was older, one could never care for earthly pleasures any more, but must care only for "Friends' meetings" and "Friends' testimonies" and "Friends' religious concerns," and must love to read the "Book of Discipline" and Barclay's "Apology" and "Friends' Religious Journals"; and must turn one's back forever upon all that was pleasant or pretty or attractive in life.

It can easily be conceived that since becoming serious meant inevitably to my mind the putting on of this awe-inspiring bonnet, it loomed before my fun-loving spirit as a fate to be unspeakably dreaded. Somehow I had gained the idea that our dear mother, in order faithfully to obey the Query about bringing up her children in "plainness of apparel," intended, when each one of her daughters reached the age of fifteen, to make them put on one of these bonnets. As a child she had herself been obliged to wear one almost from babyhood. But even her carefully trained young heart had had its moments of rebellion, for she used to tell us, as a solemn warning, that when she was nine or ten years old the girls at school made such fun of her bonnet that she became most unwilling to wear it, but no entreaties could induce her parents to consent to her leaving it off. One morning, on her way to school, as she was crossing a lonely bridge over Woodbury creek, her dislike to her little "plain bonnet" grew so strong that she took it off and kicked it before her. All day the deed weighed heavily on her conscience, and as she came to that bridge on her return home from school in the dusk of the evening, she saw a dark shadow at a little distance up the creek. To her excited imagination this shadow assumed the appearance of a threatening figure coming towards her with a fierce aspect. She firmly believed it was the Devil in person coming to snatch her to himself because of her wickedness, and, filled with terror, she flew home as fast as her trembling legs would carry her, promising in her childish heart never again to rebel against her "plain bonnet." We children were profoundly impressed with this story, and always regarded that especial bridge with the most superstitious awe; and I can remember very well many a time racing across it in breathless speed, scarcely daring to breathe for fear I should evoke the awful specter.

In the face of this experience of our mother's, I never for a moment dreamed that I could escape the fate of the "plain bonnet," and the horror with which as a child I watched my years creeping on one by one towards the fatal age of fifteen could not be described. But fortunately before I had reached that age, the subtle modification of ideas that affected the whole Society almost unconsciously, had affected our mother as well, and the dreaded "plain bonnets" never appeared on the scene. We had instead the simplest little straw cottage bonnets obtainable, but compared with the "plain bonnets" we had so dreaded, they seemed so gay and worldly to our Quaker imagination, that we felt quite like "fashionable ladies," when we walked out with them on our heads, although I am convinced now that we must have looked like the primmest little Quaker maidens possible.

When the fate, as I call it, of the "plain bonnet" fell upon any young Friend, it was generally welcomed by the older Friends with a loving tenderness that made "the cross" less hard to bear; but sometimes it would descend upon a member of a family to whom it was most unwelcome. For there were degrees of plainness among us, some being "strict" Friends, or what were oftener called "solid" Friends, while others, who indulged more in the vain fashions of the world, were called "gay" Friends. In one such frivolous family which I knew, there was a bright, lively daughter named Elizabeth, of about my own age, who went through in her early girlhood what seems to me, in looking back upon it, a tragic experience. One day when the Query about "plainness of apparel" had been read, and the usual pause had followed, a traveling Minister arose and said in an impressive manner that she believed the Lord had given her a message for some young heart present, who was called upon to take up the cross and put on the "plain dress." For some reason the young Elizabeth was profoundly impressed, and an inward voice seemed to tell her that the message was for her. She burst into a flood of tears, and at the close of the meeting one of the Elders, noticing her emotion, made her way to her side, and placing her hand upon her shoulder said solemnly, "Precious child, I believe the Lord has spoken to thee. Mayest thou be obedient to the heavenly vision." This confirmed the impression in the young Elizabeth's heart, and she went home bowed down with an awful sense of a Divine call which she felt she dared not resist.

But then began a fearful conflict. She knew her family would utterly disapprove, and she felt sure they would not give her the money to purchase the necessary articles for making the change of dress that she felt was required of her. She was afraid and ashamed to tell any one of what she was going through, and at last she decided she must try and make a "plain dress" for herself. She saved every penny of her allowance, and little by little gathered enough to purchase the cheapest materials she could find, and began at night alone in her room, after every one had gone to bed, to make with infinite labor and pains the required costume. She dared not ask for any instructions nor any patterns, and night after night, with tears and sighs, she worked at her unaccustomed task, until finally, in a rough and imperfect fashion, the poor little costume was finished, and the day came when she had to lay aside her "worldly" clothes, and appear before her family dressed in the cap and handkerchief and little drab shawl of the elderly Friends. What this cost her she would never tell me, nor could she, even in middle age, speak of, the reception she met with from her horrified family, without tears of profound pity for the martyrdom she underwent. But she said that, whether she had done right or wrong, she had at least been faithful to what she believed to be her duty, and that this had brought her such infinite peace, and the radical change in her life had been of such lasting benefit to her character, that she never wanted to lay it aside, and until the day of her death she still wore the same style of costume she had adopted in such anguish of spirit as a girl.

Perhaps an extract from my diary, shortly after my awakening at sixteen, may give a little insight into the working of these scruples upon the sensitive conscientious heart of another young girl about my own age. She was a very especial friend, and was my confidante on all religious matters.

Under date of 11/13/1849, I find the following:

"A. has been spending a week with me, and I do not know when I have enjoyed myself more. The spiritual communion between us was perfect. I do not think we concealed any of our feelings from each other. She told me of the mental suffering, suffering greater than she could have believed possible to bear, which preceded the making known of God's will in her soul, and of the anguish of spirit when that will was made known. She believed it was required of her to give up immediately all her gay dress, to burn her breastpins and her gold thimble, and many articles of clothing, and even her dresses. It was a great trial, it seemed to her so like waste, and human nature shrank. And there was a still greater trial. She had done a large picture in mono-chromatic work, which her parents had had framed and hung in their parlor, and which they greatly admired. She felt she must take this picture and burn it also with the other things, frame and all. She knew how grieved her parents would be, and how silly it would look to her sister and brother, and the conflict was very great. But the reproofs of her Divine Guide were so heartrending that at last she could bear it no longer, and submitted. Her father and mother and sister were at Cape May at the time, or she said she could not have done it. When they returned she told them; and then, she said, it was impossible for her to describe the holy, heavenly calm which followed. She scarcely felt as if she was on earth. It seemed that she should never sin again, and the reward was worth far more than the suffering. How nobly she has acted. I fear I should have refused to obey, and would have borne any suffering rather than have made so great sacrifices. And now she has consented to put on a plain bonnet—a 'sugar-scoop,' as I call them, but though it is a great change and will be much talked about, she scarcely dreads it, so true does she find it that God can make hard things easy and bitter things sweet. Could *I* take up the cross as she has done?"

That I personally must have been more or less affected by this experience of my friend is shown by an entry in my diary shortly afterwards.

"Eleventh month, 17, 1849. Sometimes to-day when I have been thinking about it, it has seemed to me almost as if it would be right for me to put on a plain sugar-scoop bonnet; but I hardly *dare* believe that so great a favor would be granted to me. It is strange, even to myself, that I have longed so for the time to come when I might make this sacrifice, though in truth it would be no sacrifice. People generally feel so averse to these bonnets, and I too did perhaps a year ago, but now I long for it so earnestly that I fear I cannot judge calmly and clearly about it; and gladly as I would make this and any other sacrifice which God might require, I know how awful it would be to run before I was sent, and to do what God had not required . . . It often seems to me that I cannot wait any longer, that I must do something to gain the salvation of my soul; and if God requires nothing, I must make offerings of my own. And yet, that I dare not do. Oh, I feel that I could love the cross and even the shame if only God would lay them upon me; but patience and quiet waiting are my duties now."

It is very evident from this extract that the martyr spirit had been aroused in me, and that I wanted to do something hard for the sake of my religion. But these feelings soon passed off, and the "sugar-scoop" bonnet I both dreaded and longed for never adorned my head. I was such a healthy young creature, and was so full of animal spirits, and so absorbed in the joys of my outward life, that my conscience was always very easily quieted; and for the most part I passed my girlhood unconscious of anything but those ordinary claims to the commonplace everyday duties of life, which my training and the compelling Quaker atmosphere around me made almost my second nature.

CHAPTER NINE

PLAINNESS OF SPEECH

*T*he "plainness of speech" referred to in the Third Query meant primarily the use of "thee" and "thou" to a single person instead of the customary "you"; and it was this "testimony" that, in conjunction with the testimony about "plainness of apparel," especially marked us off as a peculiar people. To say "you" to a single person, whether to a Friend or to an outsider, was felt to be the extreme of insincerity and worldliness, and never once, until I was married, did I dare to transgress in this respect. Of course it made it very difficult for us to mingle much with the outside world, since they would be likely to stare and laugh at our quaint language.

The reason for this testimony was no doubt to be found in the absolute sincerity of the early Quakers, who felt it to be dishonest to use a plural pronoun to a single individual; and also in the fact that, when they started, it was the custom of the world to say "you" to a superior, and to say "thee" and "thou" only to inferiors, and the Quakers, who believed all men to be free and equal, and who believed this in a very practical way, could not brook such distinctions, and felt it right to address all classes alike.

Those "early Friends" were democrats in every fiber of their beings. And this was because of their profound conviction that of one blood God had made all the nations of the earth, and that all were equally His children. It was a grand foundation upon which to build their superstructure of morals, and it accounts for many things which might otherwise seem to have been foolish fads and fancies.

In Thomas Ellwood's autobiography he gives an account of the various things he felt called upon to give up when he was convinced of Quaker views, and among them we find the following reference to this matter of the plain language.

"Again the corrupt and unsound form of speaking in the plural number to a single person, you to one person instead of thou to one, which last manner of speech has always been used by God to men, and by men to God, as well as one to another, from the oldest records of time, till corrupt men for corrupt ends, in later and corrupt times, to flatter, fawn and work upon the corrupt nature in men, brought in that false and senseless way of speaking *you* to one, which has since corrupted the modern languages, and hath greatly debased the spirits and depraved the manners of men;—this evil custom I had been as forward in as others, and this I was now called out of and required to cease from.

These and many more evil customs which had sprung up in the night of darkness and general apostasy from the truth and true religion, were now, by the inshining of this pure ray of divine light in my conscience, gradually discovered to me to be what I ought to cease from, shun, and stand a witness against."

So strongly was this testimony as to the plain language pressed upon us, that during all my childhood I felt it would have been the height of insincerity and worldliness to say "you" to a single person; it seemed to me one of the "gayest" things I could have done. And even when I became a woman, and began to go more into the world, and found that there were good and true Christians who did not hesitate to use the forbidden word in their intercourse with one another, I still found it very difficult to frame my Quaker lips to utter it. Gradually however this difficulty vanished; and now, after seventy years, the "thee" and "thou" have become to me only the language of intimate friendship, and come to me instinctively and almost unconsciously the moment a friend really finds the way to my heart. In fact I judge of the state of my feelings towards a person by this test, and when I find myself addressing them as "thee" and "thou" I know I have begun to love them. And many of my friends, who have had no connection with the Quakers, have caught the habit from me, and have themselves adopted the same dear words in our intercourse. My beloved Frances Willard was one of these, and she and I always thee'd and thou'd each other for many years before her death.

The same writer from whom I quoted before, tells in "A Boy's Religion" how he felt as a boy in regard to this "plainness of speech." He says:—

"I said 'thee' and 'thy' to everybody, and I would fully as soon have used profane words as have said 'you' or 'yours' to any one. I thought only 'Friends' went to Heaven, and so I supposed that the use of 'thee' and 'thy' was one of the main things which determined whether one would be let in or not. Nobody ever told me anything like this, and if I had asked any one at home about it, I should have had my views corrected. But for a number of years this was my settled faith.

I pitied the poor neighbors who would never be let in, and I wondered why everybody did not 'join the meeting' and learn to say 'thee' and 'thy.' I had one little Gentile friend whom I could not bear to have 'lost,' and I went faithfully to work and taught him 'the plain language,' which he always used with me until he was ten or twelve years old, when the strain of the world got too heavy upon the little fellow!"

Another "testimony" connected with "plainness of speech," which was similarly the outcome of the Quaker democracy, was against the use of "Mr." or "Mrs." or "Miss" in speaking to or of a person. These titles were considered to be a disobedience to the command of our Lord in Matt. 23:10, "Neither be ye called masters, for one is your master, even Christ." Moreover no genuine Quaker could consent to give a title to a rich man that was refused to a poor man; consequently they used their Christian names, without any prefix, to all alike; and always spoke of one another as Thomas, or Samuel, or Abigail, or Elizabeth, as the case might be. (We had no Reginalds, or Bertrands, or Ethels, or Evelyns, among us in those days!) Where a difference in age would seem to demand a little less familiarity, young people were expected to use the whole name, as Thomas Wistar, Abigail Evans, Samuel Bettle, Elizabeth Pitfield, and so on. This especial testimony was often very inconvenient when dealing with the "world's people," and it caused many awkward dilemmas. Our dear father was very strict in regard to this matter, and could never be induced, no matter how inconvenient it might be, to use the gay "Mr." or "Mrs." I remember well the fun we sometimes had, after we were grown up, over his ingenious methods of extricating himself from difficulty when he did not know the first name of anyone. He used to substitute for Mr. or Mrs. the word "Cummishilamus," and would say for instance "Cummishilamus Coleman" said or did so and so. When however he had to write the address on a letter, he could not of course use this word, and then he would turn to one of us and say, with a merry twinkle of his dear eyes,—"Come, Han, thee has no scruples, so thee may write the Mr. or Mrs. on this letter."

"Plainness of speech" also forbade our greeting our friends with good-morning or good-evening, or saying good-bye when parting from them. Good-bye was believed to be a corruption of God be with you, and, since God was always with you, it was a sort of unbelief to express a wish that He might be. And to say good-morning or good-evening, which was a form of wishing you might have a good morning or a good evening, was to express a doubt of the fact, known to every Quaker, that your mornings and your evenings must, in the order of Divine Providence, always be good. I grew up with a distinct feeling that it was very gay and worldly to use these expressions, and that the right, or in other words the "plain" thing to do was to greet my friends with, "How art thou?" or "How does thee do?" and to part from them with the simple word "Farewell." Though why "Farewell" was any more truthful than good-bye, even if good-bye did mean God be with you, I have never been able to understand.

In perfect consistence with the Quaker idea of the absolute equality of all human beings in the sight of God, "plainness of speech" forbade us to give the title of Saint to any of our departed fellow-Christians, and we were never allowed to use it, even as a prefix. We never for instance spoke of the Gospels as the Gospel according to St. Matthew, or St. Mark, or St. Luke, or St. John, but always said, "The Gospel according to Matthew," or Mark, or Luke, or John. I saw lately in an old diary kept by a Friend in the seventeenth century an account of one very conscientious Friend who felt a stop against using the prefix saint even in the names of places or streets, and who had great difficulty at one time in finding St. Mary Axe, because she dropped the Saint, and asked for it only as "Mary Axe Street," which no one understood.[1]

As a testimony against idol worship we were forbidden to call the months of the year and the days of the week by their heathen names, but were taught to keep to the "simplicity of truth" by calling them by numbers, as for instance, first month, second month, or first day, second day, etc. This was so universally observed in my circle that I do not think it ever entered my head to use the heathen names, and I remember I was greatly shocked when I came to England in 1873 to find that English Friends had given up the practice of using the numbers, and had gone back to the "heathen" names, and for a while I could hardly bring myself to feel they were really Friends at all. And even now, when I date my letters with these "heathen" names, I always feel somehow as though I were making a sort of forbidden excursion into the "forbidden world."

[1] *Friends' Examiner,* ninth month, 1902.

CHAPTER TEN

FRIENDS'
TESTIMONIES AGAINST
FICTION, MUSIC
AND ART

*A*nother point brought up in this same Third Query, which caused us great trouble was contained in the question whether Friends were careful to bring up their children in "frequently reading the Holy Scriptures, and to restrain them from reading pernicious books." All fiction of every kind was considered by the Friends of those days to be "pernicious," and on this point our mother was very strict, and we were not allowed to read even the most innocent and select Sunday-school stories. As to novels, the very word was felt to be wicked, and to this day I never use it without a momentarily instinctive feeling of lawlessness, as if I were deliberately doing something wrong.

As we grew older the line was naturally less strictly drawn; and when we became old enough to take the guidance of our lives a little more into our own hands, we would sometimes snatch a fearful joy from some storybook loaned to us by one of our school friends. One of my most vivid recollections is of such an occasion, which was made all the more vivid to me because it was the first time I had dared to partake openly and boldly of the forbidden fruit.

It was one "First Day" afternoon when there seemed to be nothing going on, I had borrowed a book from one of my schoolmates which she had told me was "lovely," and I took this book, and a plate of apples and gingerbread, and stretched myself on the outside of my bed to read and eat at my leisure.

The story I read that day, under these delightful circumstances, seemed to give me the nearest approach to perfect bliss of anything I had ever before experienced, and it remains in my memory as one of the happiest days of my life. The book was "The Earl's Daughter," by Grace Aguilar, and to my young American and Quaker mind an Earl was more like an archangel than a man, and to be an Earl's daughter was almost akin to being a daughter of heaven. And to this day, in spite of all the disillusions that life has brought me about earls and their daughters, the old sense of grandeur that filled my soul with awe on that First Day afternoon so long ago, never fails to come back for at least a moment, when earls and countesses are mentioned in my presence.

But although I enjoyed this and other stories intensely, it was always with an uneasy conscience, and it took me fifty years to get rid of the feeling that to read anything fictitious was to commit a sin. My diary is full of the conflicts I went through on account of this, and, as I read them over, I cannot but feel a real pity for the hungry, ignorant young soul that was so tormented by the constant tendency to make a sin out of a perfectly innocent recreation. The thing that at last brought me deliverance was a sudden recognition of the fact that our Lord Himself constantly used parables, which were only another name for stories, to illustrate and enforce His teaching, and that therefore fiction was not in itself, as I had always thought, a synonym for sin, but that its sinfulness depended entirely upon the sort of fiction it was; and that often fiction might be found to be an invaluable aid to virtue. But I have known many Friends who have been tormented by scruples on this point up to old age.

Music was another thing against which the Friends of my day had a very strong testimony. In a book of Discipline, published in Philadelphia in 1873, I have found the following passage in regard to it, which gives the Quaker idea concerning it.

"We would renewedly caution all our members against indulging in music, or having instruments of music in their houses, believing that the practice tends to promote a light and vain mind, and to disqualify for the serious thoughtfulness, which becomes an accountable being, hastening to his final reckoning. . . . The spirit and language of the discipline forbid the use of music by Friends, without any exception in favor of that called sacred, and in order to produce harmonious action on this subject throughout the subordinate meetings, the yearly meeting instructs them that those members who indulge in the use of music, or who have musical instruments in their houses, bring themselves within the application of this second clause of the Discipline, viz.: 'And if any of our members fall into either of these practices, and are not prevailed with, by private labor to decline them, the monthly meeting to which the offenders belong should be informed thereof, and if they be not reclaimed by further labor so as to condemn their misconduct to the satisfaction of the meeting, it should proceed to testify our disunity with them.'" 1873.

So strictly was the Discipline obeyed in this respect that I do not remember in my young days a single individual in our select circle who owned any sort of musical instrument, and above all a piano, which was considered the gayest of the gay. And when it chanced that I found myself in a strange room containing a piano, I always felt as if I were treading the very borders of hell. For many years after I was a woman I never heard any music anywhere that I did not have a secret half-delicious sensation of tasting forbidden fruit. Even singing or whistling were frowned down upon. I remember once when a party of young Quakers were all together at Newport for a summer holiday, a dear old Friend called them into his room, and told them solemnly that he had been very much grieved to hear some of them whistling in the garden the day before, and he hoped they would not so transgress Friends' testimonies again.

That the Discipline in this matter was no dead letter is proved by the fact that when I was older and this testimony was more or less losing its power over the less "concerned" members, I knew of several instances where Friends, who, though otherwise exemplary, were not strict in the matter of music, were actually turned out of membership for having a piano in their houses. And as late as 1865 when we had presented our son Frank with a cottage organ (we did not dare to let it be a piano, as we felt organs were for some reason "plainer" than pianos), we were obliged to hide it in one of the top rooms of our house, in order to spare the feelings of our Quaker relations. I never shall forget my surprise when I first waked up to the fact that musical instruments were not only sanctioned in the Bible, but that we were actually commanded to use them. In reading the Psalms one day I could hardly believe my eyes when I came across Psalm 150 and read, "Praise ye the Lord. . . . Praise Him with the sound of the trumpet, praise Him with the psaltery and harp. Praise Him with the timbrel and dance: praise Him with stringed instruments and organs." I never heard any Friend explain how they got over this.

"Plainness" in my day also excluded pictures everywhere, except in books. No good Quakers would have any pictures on their walls, nor did they feel free to have their pictures taken. Even daguerreotypes, when they came in, were considered frivolous by all the really good Friends. I believe they had an idea that pictures of oneself might tend to vanity. And for some occult reason it seemed to be felt that pictures or statuary were dangerous, as offering a temptation to idolatry. I certainly grew up believing that it was wicked to go to picture galleries, or to look at a statue. And I remember well, when I was about seventeen, breaking loose from all the traditions of my life, and going with a beating heart, as though on some perilously wicked excursion, into the Academy of Fine Arts in Philadelphia. There was a marble group there of Hero and Leander, and I am afraid Leander had not many clothes on, and I can see myself now, standing and looking at it with my heart in my mouth, and saying to myself, "I suppose now I shall go straight to hell, but I cannot help it. If I must go there I must, but I *will* look at this statue." No words can express what a daring sinner I felt myself to be; and I remember distinctly that I was quite surprised to find myself safely outside that Academy, standing unharmed in Broad Street, without having experienced the swift judgments of an offended Creator.

I can see that marble group vividly even to this day, far more vividly than any statuary I have ever seen since; and although I do not suppose it was all what would be called good art nowadays, yet to me it has always lived in my memory as the acme of all art, for it was my emancipation into the hitherto absolutely unknown art world. Nothing dreadful happened to me from looking at this, and I gradually gained courage for more, until at last I learned that a gift for art was as much a Divine bestowment as a gift for mathematics, and as such it could not be wrong to develop and exercise it. And gradually the Friends also have seemed to learn this, and those old scruples against art and music have almost entirely vanished from there midst.

Another testimony included in "plainness of apparel" in my young days was one against beards. It happened that when Friends' customs began to crystallize, smooth faces were universal; and, as a consequence, with the Friends' idea of not following the changing fashions, when beards began to be fashionable, Quakers kept on with their smooth faces. As the fashion for beards became more insistent, the Quakers took a firmer and firmer stand, until insensibly, without any real reason for it that I ever heard, it developed into a "religious testimony"; and when I was born into the Society it was one of the most stringent. I remember vividly the first time I saw a "preacher" wearing his beard. He was a visiting Friend from England, where they were less strict, and, in spite of the fact that I had a great reverence for English Friends, his beard seemed to me so evidently the mark of the evil one, that I felt it almost a sin to listen to his preaching. In several "strict" Meetings this same preacher was refused entrance to the "gallery" because of his beard; and I can remember well the great concern expressed by the Philadelphia Elders over this sad evidence of the "gradual encroachments of a world spirit in London Yearly Meeting."

This testimony against beards is shared, I believe, though probably on different grounds, by the Roman Catholic priests, and also by High Church clergymen of the Church of England. But the Friends meanwhile have dropped it, along with many others of the strict testimonies of my childhood. They still practice great moderation in their dress and address, and in the furnishing of their houses, and the ordering of their lives, but they have for the most part abandoned all idea of any especial cut of clothes, or any stifling of natural gifts, either in literature, or art, or music, being a necessary passport to the favor of heaven. But one cannot but admire and reverence the sturdy adherence to what was felt to be a religious duty, even though it may seem to us a mistaken duty, which characterized those dear old saints.

CHAPTER ELEVEN

QUAKER SCRUPLES

*T*he individual "scruples" resulting from the various "testimonies" of which I have spoken were practically endless, for
each individual would of course interpret and apply them according
to their own convictions of duty; and morbidly conscientious souls
would be continually inventing new scruples, until life to some of
them often became almost a torment. One of my friends, who had
inherited a particularly morbid conscience, told me, after we were
middle-aged women, that no words could express what she went
through on this account when she was younger. She said that often
it seemed impossible for her to get dressed and downstairs in the
morning because of the "scruples" that beset her about every article
of her clothing, and that the only way she could sometimes manage
it at all was by stuffing her ears with cotton, and repeating over, as
fast as she could, extracts of poetry, so as to keep herself from hearing the inward voice that was continually urging her to fresh sacrifices.

In a diary kept by an old great-grandmother of our family in the
years 1760 to 1762 there is a very quaint and vivid picture of the
"scruples" which the Quakerism of her day had engendered in an

earnest but narrow-minded soul. In one place she writes as follows:—

"Solomon said of laughter, 'It is madness,' and of mirth, 'What doeth it?' for even in laughter the heart is sorrowful and the end of that mirth is heaviness. I often think if I could be so fixed as never to laugh nor to smile, I should be one step better. It fills me with sorrow when I see people so full of laugh."

Again she writes bemoaning the lax condition of things among the Quakers of her day:

"Oh! will there ever be a Nehemiah raised at our meeting? Oh! the fashions and running into them; the young men wearing of their hats set up behind; next it must be a ribbon to tie their hair behind. The girls in Pennsylvania have got their necks set off with a black ribbon—a sorrowful sight indeed. But what did that dear friend, Nicholas Davis, tell them—the old people had not done their duty, and that was the reason the young were no better. Six of those girls from Darby were here from John Hunt's. I thought they did not belong to Friends till I was informed they did. But I many times think what signifies my being concerned about fashions. Where is one Friend's child or children but some doddery fashion or another is on their backs or their heads? Here is this day Josiah Albason's son, all the son he has, with his hat close up behind."

Again under date of 3/18/1762, she writes:

"Oh! lamentable is our case I think I am so filled with sorrow many times about the wicked. Oh, I think could my eyes run down with tears always at the abominations of the times— so much excess of tobacco, and tea is as bad, so much of it, and they will pretend they can't do without it. And there is the calico. Oh! the calico! We pretend to a plain dress and plain speech, but where is our plainness? Ain't we like all the rest, be they who they will? What fashion have not the Quakers got? As William Hunt said, 'Oh! that we had many such as he, or enough such; there would be no calico among the Quakers, no, nor so many fashion-mongers. I think tobacco, and tea, and calico may all be set down, all one as bad as another.'"

Those extracts from my great-grandmother's diary show plainly that the scruples of one generation were not always the scruples of another; but in every case the spirit of self-denial was the same.

Another grandmother, nearer to me in time, whom I can well remember, felt a scruple against false teeth. They were just beginning to be used, and as she was toothless from old age, and had great difficulty in eating, my father had persuaded her to have a set made. But when they came home she told us that she "felt a stop" in her mind about wearing them, as they seemed to her to be of the vain fashions of the world. They were consequently put away in a drawer with her best silk shawl, and never saw the light again. I remember well how saintly we young people felt the dear old lady to be, as we watched her difficulty in eating, and her necessary refusal of so much that we thought good.

A dear friend who lived near us when I was a child, and who was a preacher in our Meeting, bought herself a new parlor carpet and had it laid down, and then became so afraid lest she had allowed pride to enter, that she felt "led" to have several wheelbarrow loads of rough stones dumped out upon it in order to take off its freshness. We children heard the story of it all with an awe not to be described, and from that time the preaching of this dear saint seemed to us like the voice of an angel from Heaven.

I cannot help contrasting here an experience of my own over a new carpet many years afterwards, when I had learned something of the life of faith, and knew the power of Christ to deliver. We had just bought a new Brussels carpet for our drawing-room, with delicate sprigs of flowers all over it, and I was very proud and pleased. Shortly after it was put down, my husband arranged to have a number of rough workingmen come every Sunday morning to this very drawing-room for a Bible class. It was a great trial to me to have my carpet used in that way, and I was inclined to resent it, but I ought not to feel so, and yet I did not exactly see how to overcome the feeling. Some one happened to say to me about that time that there was always some passage in Scripture which would help you out of every difficulty. This impressed me, and once when I was praying about my carpet difficulty I said to myself, "Well, I am certain that there is no Scripture anywhere that says anything about drawing-room carpets"; when at that very moment there flashed into my mind the passage, "Take joyfully the spoiling of your goods." I immediately seized hold of that word of God as the Sword of the Spirit with which to conquer my enemy, and from that moment rather enjoyed seeing those rough men tramp over my new carpet. And I may say in conclusion that that carpet seemed as if it never would wear out. It lasted for years, until I was quite tired of the sight of it. I cannot help thinking mine was a better way than the rough stones of the dear old Friend.

After I had discovered this way of faith one of my friends who had suffered much from the Quaker "Scruples," gave me a striking analysis of the different methods of living the Christian life. She said, "I have noticed that there are three ways of getting to the other side of a spiritual mountain. Some people tunnel through by the sweat of their brows, and that is the Quaker way, and was for a long time my way. Some meander around the base of the mountain, going this way and that, but, because they always keep their faces turned towards the goal, they gradually, in spite of their meanderings, draw nearer and nearer to the other side; and this," she said, "was the way I adopted when I was worn out with my tunneling. But now," she added, "here you are telling me that there is a third way, which is far better than either of the others, and that is the way of faith. You say that there are Christians who have found out that they can just flap the wings of faith and fly right over the mountain, and you declare that this is the way you adopt. I must confess that the people who adopt your way seem to get to the other side far more quickly and more easily than those who tunnel or those who meander, and I have decided to give up all tunneling and all meandering, and to flap my wings too and go over."

But the dear old saints, among whom my childhood and girlhood were passed, did not seem to know how to flap their wings; and for the most part they spent their lives in steadfast though weary tunneling. But their faithfulness and self-sacrifice, even though I may feel it was in mistaken ways, seemed then and seems now to have been worthy of all honor. And the one strong overmastering impression that it all made upon my young heart was simply this—that, by hook or by crook, I had *got* to be good. No matter what lack of religious teaching there may have been in other directions among the Philadelphia Quakers, there was no lack here. The supreme and paramount necessity of being good—thoroughly and honestly and genuinely good—was in the very air we breathed, and almost in the very food we ate.

I confess that I sometimes chafed at this. The adventurous nature in me now and then pined for a chance to be naughty—to do something I ought not to do, or to leave undone something that was expected of me—but the limitations of my life made only very innocent naughtiness possible. And in looking back upon it now I am forced to admire the wonderful atmosphere of goodness that surrounded me with such a sure defense against the evil that would otherwise I feel certain, have been so enticing to a wild free nature like mine. For if any human being was ever born free I was. The one cry of my soul has always been for freedom. "Bonds that enslave and tyrannies that fetter" have always been my abhorrence, whether they were bonds of actual rules, or merely bonds of conventional custom. Had my parents made many rules, I should have been driven to disobey them, but the all enveloping atmosphere of goodness, in which they and their circle lived and moved, controlled and constrained my wayward spirit with such unconscious power, that I hardly knew I was being controlled, and had a blissful feeling that somehow I nearly always had my own way.

No one, who did not live in it, could I feel sure, conceive of the narrow range of life with which I was acquainted up to the age of eighteen. I never met anybody who lived in what was called "the gay world." My associates were only the staid, sober "Friends" of our little circle, and their carefully guarded children. I never, as I have said, was allowed to read any novels; and I had absolutely no opportunity of learning what life meant outside of our narrow Quaker fold. As to the sin of the world I had not the slightest inkling. Nobody ever told me anything, not even the girls at school; or, if they did, I was too utterly ignorant and innocent to understand them; I venture to say that it would be perfectly impossible in the present day for a girl of eighteen to live in such an unreal world of ignorance as the one in which I lived, or to enter upon the responsibilities of life more absolutely unprepared to meet them.

My interior life up to the age of sixteen was of the simplest. I believed what I was told, which however I have shown was very little, and troubled myself not one whit about the problems of the universe. My only conscious religious thoughts were an underlying fear of hell-fire, which now and then sprang into active life when any epidemic was abroad or any danger seemed to threaten. How I came to have this fear I cannot now remember, for the Quakers rarely touched on the future life in any way, either as regarded heaven or hell. Their one concern was as to the life of God in the soul of man now and here, and they believed that where this was realized and lived, the future could be safely left in the Divine care. But now and then I would get a sudden fright in regard to my future and would make tremendous resolutions about "being good" and would for a few hours really try to correct my faults. But such occasions were not very lasting, and I would soon relapse into the old unthinking ways.

As I have said, however, the atmosphere in which I lived was so impregnated with goodness that it was not easy even to think of anything naughty, much less to come to the point of actually doing it, and I believe I may fairly say that on the whole I was as good as a creature full of energy and high spirits, and with bouncing health, could be expected to be. But up to the age of sixteen I was simply a good animal. My spiritual nature was unawakened, and I had never consciously been made aware of the existence of my soul.

But a change was at hand, although I little knew it. My soul was awaking from its torpor, and, like the butterfly in the cocoon, was struggling to escape from the bonds that had hitherto held it in leash. My long search after God was about to begin.

CHAPTER TWELVE

My Awakening

*I*n my religious life several epochs stand out clearly before me. The first one dawned as I have said when I was sixteen. In a dim mysterious way I began to be filled with vague longings after something that would satisfy my interior nature. In my diary of the autumn of 1848 I find records of these longings, and of a blind reaching out for something to fill what I called in the tragic language of youth "the aching void in my heart." In the midst of this I fell head over ears in love with one of the young teachers in the school I was attending, and her influence changed my life. I find a record in my diary of all the steps of my acquaintance with her—of my longings to speak to her and to beg for her love, and of my hesitation for fear of bothering her. I write about it as follows:

"1848. Sixteen years old. This is an important time for me. Now is the forming time of my character. I feel as I never felt before. The great and solemn duties of life have, for the first

time come before me. I was not born to be an idler, for I feel
something within me, which tells me—

> " 'Life has imports more inspiring
>   Than the fancies of thy youth;
> It has hopes as high as heaven
>   It has labor, it has truth.
> It has wrongs that may be righted,
>   Noble deeds that may be done.
> Its great battles are unfought
>   Its great triumphs are unwon.'

"Something which points onwards, far onwards into the future, beyond this into a brighter, happier world, and tells me
of the glorious reward of those who fulfill their duties. I have
not felt this long:—three months ago I was a careless, happy
child. I am still a child, but an earnest reflecting one, no
longer careless or indifferent. How can I be so, when there is
so much, so very much to be thought about; and *so much* to be
done? What has caused this change? Then there was an aching
void in my heart. I felt a want of something, something I
knew not what, something indefinable which would cause me
to sit dreamily for hours and look into the sky, and watch the
pale stars or the moon, until my very being seemed merged
into theirs and I almost forgot I was on earth, while my
thoughts wandered far off to the pathless regions over which
they presided, and I would strive in vain to pierce the mysteries of their existence. Study, I thought, would fill that void,
but I found I was mistaken. In such a state was my mind
when, in the beginning of ninth month we left our darling little
cottage home and returned to the city. If I had then met with
one whom I could have loved but whose principles were bad,
I shudder to think what would have been the consequences,
for I am very easily influenced by those I love. But my Heavenly Father was willing to extend a little mercy towards me.
He sent across my path one in whom I found a *true friend*.
She was a young girl employed by Miss Maryanna as compo-
sition teacher named Anna S—. I was prepared to love her
even before I saw her, for one whom I love had told me of her
loveliness. For two weeks after she first came to school I

never spoke to her, I believe, but once; and then I saw her looking for a book and handed one to her asking if that was the right one. I thought we never would get acquainted. I used to sit and watch her and wish I dare speak to her and kiss her, and this very longing made me particularly retiring. I would see her put her arms around other girls, and I would turn away in sorrow to think she would not do the same to me. At last one day, how well I remember it, I was standing at my desk when she came up and spoke about A.S.F. How happy I felt! How I longed to throw my arms around her neck and beg her to let me love her! My heart was all in a tumult, yet I answered her calmly and without emotion and she soon left me. However the ice was broken, we began to speak more frequently, and one morning she kissed me. That kiss was engraven on my heart. I felt that she loved me, and the thought was happiness. From that moment I have loved, nay almost idolized her. The aching void in my heart now is partly filled, for I have listened to her sentiments, I have seen her noble principles of action, and I have found that 'life is real, life is earnest,' and is not to be passed in idle dreaming, or wasted in frivolous amusements. She has taught me, not in so many words but quietly, by her influence, that I have a mission to fulfill on earth, and straightway I must set to work to perform it. That henceforward I must struggle earnestly to become pure and holy and noble-hearted that I may be great in the world and perform faithfully my part in the great battle of life. Her influence has aroused me from my dream of childhood. In one short month I have become a woman. Oh! how blessed has her friendship been to me! I hope, earnestly hope I may not abuse the privilege."

A day or two later I wrote:—

"Every day I feel grateful to my Heavenly Father for blessing me with such a friend as Anna. This is such an important period of my life. I tremble when I think of the awful responsibility resting upon me. My character is forming, and I have power to be what I choose. Oh, may I choose to be a good and noble woman! To-day, as I walked along the street and thought of what might be my future destiny, it made me almost shrink. I may be destined for some great work. I feel that within me which tells me I could accomplish it. At any rate I shall do a great deal of good or evil. I *will* choose the former. Oh, my Father who art in Heaven, wilt Thou not assist me to advance in the path of self-conquest, which must be my first great battle. What a glorious triumph it will be if I succeed!"

According to my diary, every day now seemed to awaken my spiritual nature more and more, until at last a sort of climax arrived, and on 11/28/1848, I wrote:

"An eventful day! Eventful I mean in my spiritual life. Today I have felt and thought enough for a year. My friend Anna read to us in class a book called 'Other Worlds,' and also 'Future Existence,' from the 'School Boy,' by Abbott. It was all intensely interesting, and had an almost overpowering effect on me. As I listened to the accounts of those mighty worlds which are everywhere scattered around us, some of which are so distant that the rays of light from them which enter our eyes have left these stars six thousand years ago! As I reflected that these worlds were all moving on regularly, never disturbing each other, but all obedient to one mighty Creator, the grandeur of the thought was intense, and for a few minutes I felt as though the happiness of being born into a universe so limitless, so magnificent, so glorious, was too great. And as I heard of our future existence, of the glorious unimaginable happiness in store for us, of the perfect bliss of the good and holy, I inwardly thanked my Creator for placing me among beings whose anticipations were so happy. But then came the awful, the overwhelming thought that that eternity of endless bliss was only for the good, and the remembrance that I could have no share in it unless my heart was changed. Oh, I cannot describe the misery of that moment! It was almost too great to be borne. And these thoughts linger with me. Why is it?"

The impression made upon me by this glimpse, as it were, into the magnificence of the universe has never to this day left me. At the bottom of all my questionings about God there has always been a conviction of His illimitable power which nothing would ever be able to withstand. But for a long time, as will be seen, I thought of this power as being a selfish power, engaged, not on my side, but against me; and my one question for many years was as to how I could win the God who possessed it over to my side.

My awakening had come in earnest! I was then about sixteen-and-a-half, and from that time onwards my soul was athirst to make myself worthy of the glorious destiny of which I seemed to have had a glimpse. And even deeper than this was the longing to become acquainted with the God who had created the unimaginable wonders of which I had been reading. I have no recollection of any especial trouble about my sins. It was the magnificence of God that had enthralled me, and I felt as if it would be the grandest thing in life to come to know Him. And then and there my search began. But alas! what a blind and ignorant search it was at first.

My only confidante was my friend Anna ————. Not for the world would I have said anything to my parents on the subject. Their Quaker habits of reserve on all matters of religion seemed to make it impossible. But to my friend, after this day of awakening, I poured out my heart in a long letter full of my aspirations and my yearnings. In my diary I have a copy of her reply with the following comments.

"Anna wrote me a little note in reply to my letter. Never had I received one which thrilled me more stirringly than that! She begged me to give up all to my Savior, to pray for strength, and to strive earnestly after holiness no matter what it may cost me. 'Oh dearest Hannah,' she said, 'do let us try. Let us seek to journey together towards His glorious kingdom! Let us struggle for a portion of His Spirit.'

"Oh that I could follow her advice! I sat here alone in my study and tried to feel as if I could give up all. But I could not. I could not even feel repentance for the many, many sins I have committed; and, far worse than all, I could not feel as if I really loved God. It is dreadful. What shall I do? I must repent, I must love my Heavenly Father, or I shall be eternally ruined. But I cannot do it of myself; God alone can help me, and I know not how to pray. Oh what shall I do? Where shall I go? It is said, 'Ask, and ye shall receive.' But I cannot become really righteous until I repent, and I cannot repent."

From this time onward my religious diary is one long record of wrestlings and agonizings, with scarcely a ray of light. My friend did her best to help me, but she, like myself, supposed that the only way to find God was to search for Him within. Our Quaker education had been as I have shown to refer us under all circumstances to the "light within" for teaching and guidance, and we believed that only when God should reveal Himself there, could we come really to know Him. In an old Quaker tract which I have found among my papers, called, "What shall we do to be saved?" there is a passage that sets forth clearly the sort of teaching with which we had grown up. It is as follows:

"I cannot direct the searcher after truth who is pensively enquiring what he shall do to be saved, to the ministry of any man; but would rather recommend him to the immediate teaching of the word nigh in the heart, even the Spirit of God. This is the only infallible teacher, and the primary adequate rule of faith and practice: it will lead those who attend to its dictates into the peaceable paths of safety and truth. 'Ye need not,' said the Apostle to the Church formerly, 'that any man teach you, save as this anointing teacheth, which is truth and no lie.'"

The natural result of this teaching was to turn our minds inward, upon our feelings and our emotions, and to make us judge of our relations with God entirely by what we found within ourselves. What God had said in the Bible seemed to us of not nearly so much authority as what He might say to us in our own hearts, and I have no recollection of ever for a moment going to the Scriptures for instruction. The "inward voice" was to be our sole teacher. And for me at that time the inward voice meant only my own feelings and my own emotions. As there is absolutely nothing more unreliable and unmanageable than one's inward feelings, it is no wonder that I plunged into a hopeless struggle. In vain I tried to work myself up into what I supposed would be the sort of feelings acceptable to God. No dream of salvation in any other way ever came to me. I talked about "my Savior," as I called Him, but I never for a moment even so much as imagined that He could or would save me unless I could make myself worthy to be saved; and as this worthiness was mostly, I believed, a matter of inward pious emotions, I had no thought but to try somehow to get up these emotions. Any one who has ever tried to do this will know what a weary, hopeless task it was. The records in my diary of my religious life from the age of sixteen onwards are a sad illustration of the false methods of religion which were all I knew. As I read them over I cannot but pity the eager, hungry soul that was reaching out so vainly after light, but found only confusion and darkness.

One thing however consoles me in this retrospect, and that is that none of these religious struggles seem, as far as I can remember, to have darkened the skies of my outward happiness. My times for attending to my religious life were either in our Quaker Meetings, or when I was alone in my study during the twilight, or at night after every one else had gone to bed, and all the tragic records in my diary were written then; while throughout the day I was generally too happy and too full of interests in my outward life to be troubled by what went on in my religious seasons. I feel that this was a great cause for thankfulness, for had the struggles I went through in our silent Meetings or in my hours of meditation extended through the days as well, I do not like to think of what might have been the consequences. I believe my diary was my safety valve, for I can remember well, that, after writing there the most tragic and despairing records, I would somehow feel as if my religious exercises were over, and would go off to bed quite happily, and sleep the sleep of the just without a moment of wakeful anxiety or worry, and would wake up the next morning full of the joys of a new day, forgetting all the miseries I had so despairingly recorded the night before. I was, I recollect, now and then rather surprised at this easy transition, and find the following in my diary during this time:

"I cannot understand my feelings. Such a hungering and thirsting after righteousness, and yet, except in a few moments of retirement (when I write in my diary), such lightness, and gaiety, and indifference. It seems to me almost wrong to laugh, and yet I indulge in it continually. . . .

"I know not how God can look upon me even in pity, I am *so* wicked. So often have I entered into a covenant to serve Him wholly and entirely, with fervor of spirit, but when the impression of my hours of retirement has nearly faded, and the temptations of the world have assailed me, I have yielded, and have forgotten my high and holy calling through fear of the world's dread laugh, and through the love of sin. Oh that I could do otherwise! The mercy of God will some day be exhausted, and where will I be then? I dare not think."

I can see now that it was, as I have said, my salvation from an utterly morbid false sort of religion, that my natural happy joyousness continually delivered me out of its snares, although at the time this seemed to me so wicked. How morbid and false all my ideas of religion were at this time, a few further extracts from my diary will reveal.

"Oh it is a sorrowful thought that upon myself depends the salvation of my soul, and I can do absolutely nothing! Whichever side I turn all looks dark and gloomy. Oh I must renew my efforts. . . . Oh that I could repent! But I cannot. I know it is wrong, I dread the anger of God, but I cannot feel what I know true repentance is. Oh that I could! I almost wish I could be as indifferent as I once was, that I could forget all that I have felt; for it seems impossible for me ever to be a Christian. . . .

"This afternoon in meeting I was favored to feel, more perhaps than ever before, the spirit of supplication. My exercise was so great that I could scarcely sit still. My head throbbed painfully, and my heart felt as though it would break with the agony. Oh how awful to feel that I have of myself no power even to think a holy thought, and yet I must gain the salvation of my soul. I cannot repent, I cannot love my Savior, and I do not believe I ever will. What, what shall I do?"

Three months after my awakening I wrote:

"It has been more than three months since I began in earnest to seek the salvation of my soul, and I have not advanced one step. Could I have seen then all that was before me I should have given up in despair. I should have thought it impossible to wait and pray and struggle for three months, and gain nothing. Now I look forward to many, many more months of prayer, and struggling, and waiting, with a fear, almost a certainty, that that too will be all in vain. If there was only some outward work, entirely distinct from the inward change which is necessary, something to be *done,* not something to be prayed for—a cutting off of a hand or a foot, or inflicting austerities upon myself, then perhaps I might become a Christian, for such things I *could* do. But the inward change I cannot effect, and yet I am accountable if it is not

130

effected. Accountable for not doing what I cannot do! It is a dreadful thought! I feel just as if I was seated, sick and weary, at the base of a high and inaccessible mountain peak, whose summit I must reach alone in the darkness of night. Oh Heavenly Father, wilt Thou not enable me to be faithful, to strive earnestly, and to endure to the end. . . . I am so ignorant and inexperienced that I feel almost afraid to do anything. There are many, many things I long to enquire about, but whom shall I ask? I cannot speak to my parents until I know of a certainty that I am accepted. I love them too dearly to be willing to cause the anguish of seeing me give up in despair. My own dear friend, Anna, says she is not a Christian, and she dare not counsel or comfort me. And there is no one. Alone I must bear all my burdens! Alone I must seek the entrance to the straight and narrow way! Alone I must work out my soul's salvation! And I can of myself do nothing! Oh what shall I do?"

As an illustration of the sort of teaching I was receiving at this time the following extract will be valuable:

"Went to 12th Street meeting this morning, where I was favored to have a few moments of real prayer. But my discouragement was very great, so that I could scarcely avoid crying aloud for help; and in my despair I besought my Father in Heaven, if it seemed good unto Him, to put a few words of encouragement into the mouth of one of His servants. My prayer was answered. Almost immediately Samuel Bettle rose and spoke in a manner remarkably applicable to me, bidding the poor and needy, though now they might seem to be in the depths of tribulation, in darkness and seeing no light, and thirsty yet finding no water, to put their trust in the Lord Jesus, and patiently abide His time, and they would be filled with the light of His Holy Spirit, and fountains of living water would flow from them freely."

Of what it meant to "put one's trust in Jesus" I had not the faintest conception, and I do not remember giving it a moment's thought. But to "patiently abide God's time" seemed something I could understand, and I went home from the meeting that day with a weary sense of an interminable waiting for the light of the Holy Spirit to shine in my heart and give me the longed-for joy and peace. And so day after day went by in a hopeless watching of my feelings and my emotions, which I was never able to bring up to the right pitch of fervor; and my unrest and darkness of spirit only grew more and more despairing.

One final extract from my diary will suffice.

"3/11/1849. Very sad. The fear that this longing for salvation may be all a delusion attends me always, and everything is so completely veiled in gloom that I can scarcely take a single step. It seems to me I cannot bear this state much longer. But oh Father! Thy will not mine be done."

CHAPTER THIRTEEN

ECLIPSE OF FAITH

*T*his morbid self-introspection lasted, with variable degrees of earnestness, until the time of my marriage at nineteen. Nothing ever came of it, and in the nature of things, nothing ever could. It was a self-involved religion that had no relation whatever to any Divine facts. And I see now that it was a mercy my marriage, and the new life and wider interests into which I was introduced, more or less turned my attention in other directions, and made my religious emotions and feelings sink into the background for a time, so that my mind became free at a later period to take an entirely different view of the religious life.

I believe, however, that my experiences during these years have been valuable in one way, and that is in teaching me to avoid ever encouraging in the young people I have known any sort of a self-absorbed interior life. Self-absorption is always a temptation to young people, and if their religion is of a sort to add to this self-absorption, I feel that it is a serious mistake. If I had my way, the whole subject of feelings and emotions in the religious life would be absolutely ignored. Feelings there will be, doubtless, but they must not be in the least depended on, nor in any sense be taken as the test or gauge of one's religion. They ought to be left out of the calculation entirely. You may feel good or you may feel bad, but neither the good feeling nor the bad feeling affects the real thing. It may affect your comfort in the thing, but it has nothing to do with the reality of the thing. If God loves you, it is of no account, as far as the fact goes, whether you feel that He loves you or do not feel it; although, as I say, it materially affects your comfort. Of course, if you really believe that He loves you, you cannot help being glad about it; but if you make your belief dependent upon your feelings of gladness, you are reversing God's order in the most hopeless kind of way. I like so much that story of Luther when the devil said to him: "Luther, do you feel that you are a child of God?" and Luther replied, "No, I do not *feel* it at all, but I *know* it. Get thee behind me, Satan."

During all the years when I was struggling over my feelings, I never succeeded in making them what I thought they ought to be; and as a consequence the religious part of my life was a misery to me. But after I had learned that the facts of religion were far more important than my feelings about these facts, and had consequently given up looking at my feelings, and sought only to discover the facts, I became always happy in my religious life, and had, without any effort, the very feelings of love to God, and of rest and peace and joy in my soul that before I had so vainly tried to work up. No words can express how vital I consider this point to be, nor how much, since I have found it out for myself, I have longed to make everybody else see it.

Many years after it had all become clear to me, one of my children came to me evidently in great perplexity and said, "Mother, how long does it take God to forgive you when you have been naughty?" "It does not take Him a minute," I replied. "Oh," she said, "I can't believe that. I think you have to feel sorry first for a good many days, and then you have to ask Him in a very pretty and nice way, and then perhaps He can forgive you." "But," I said, "daughter, the Bible says that if we confess our sins He is faithful and just to forgive us right straight off." "Well," she said, "I wouldn't believe that if fifty Bibles said it, because I know that you have got to feel sorry for quite a good while, and then you have got to ask God in a very pretty way, and then you have got to wait till He is ready to forgive you."

I found the case was really serious, so, taking the child on my lap, I opened the Bible and made her read out loud the verse I had quoted, and then explained to her that God loved us so much that He sent His Son to die for us, and that, because of His love, He was always ready to forgive us the minute we asked Him, just as mothers were always ready to forgive their children as soon as the children wanted to be forgiven. At last the child was convinced, and putting her little hands together she said in a reverent little voice, "Dear Lord Jesus, I want you to forgive me this very minute for all my naughty, and I am certain sure you will, because you love me." And then she jumped down off my lap and ran away shouting merrily in childish glee.

My little girl was happy because she had found out a happy fact and believed it. But in her first way of looking at the matter she was only voicing the natural idea of the human heart. We all feel, as she did, that we must come to God with great doubt and timidity, as to a Being of whom we know but little, and whom we fear much; and that His favor depends altogether upon the beauty and suitableness of our emotions, and the ceremonious order of our approach. To come "boldly to the throne of grace to find mercy and obtain help in the time of need" is only possible to the soul that has been brought into a real acquaintance with the goodness of God.

During all the years however of which I speak, from the age of sixteen to twenty-six, I knew nothing of this. God was to me a far off, unapproachable Being, whom, in spite of all my eager and painful searching, I failed utterly to find. I had not the slightest conception of what the expression "God is love" meant. My idea of Him was that He was a stern and selfish taskmaster, who might perhaps, if one could only secure the sort of feelings and of conduct that would please Him, be induced to pay some little attention to the needs of His children, but who was for the most part so absorbed in thoughts of His own glory, and of the consideration and reverence due to Himself, that it was almost impossible, except by a superhuman degree of perfection, to win His regards. He seemed to me a supremely selfish Autocrat who held my fate in His hands, but who only cared for me in proportion to my power of adding to His honor and His glory. Of all His loving and beautiful unselfishness, which I was afterwards to discover, I had for all these years not the faintest glimpse.

Moreover, the only way I knew of by which one could know that this unapproachable Diety did condescend to turn even a slight ear to the cries of His children, was to have some sort of an interior feeling of it, and consequently, whenever I was religious at all, the whole energy of my spirit was spent, as I have said, in the effort to acquire in some occult way this necessary inward feeling. The sort of introspection I had imbibed from my Quaker teaching was calculated to lead to constant self-examination, not so much into one's actions, as into one's emotions! And, considering what ticklish things our emotions are, and how much they depend upon the state of our health, or the state of the weather, or the influence of other minds, no more fatal occupation in my opinion can be indulged in than this sort of self-examination, and no more unreliable gauge could possibly be found as to one's spiritual condition than that afforded by one's own interior emotions. But the religion of my years between sixteen and twenty-six was nothing but a religion of trying to feel; and, as I was a very natural, healthy sort of being, my feelings were not likely to be very sentimental or pious; and the agonizing futile efforts that I have described to bring them up to the right religious pitch is something pitiful to consider.

My soul hungered after God, but I could not find Him. Even the comfort of prayer was denied me, for I had, as I have said, imbibed the idea that you could not pray acceptably unless you felt an inward sense of the Divine favor, and that any prayers offered without this sense were really a mockery, and even perhaps a sin. And, since this inward sense of God's favor was the very thing I was seeking to secure, and yet might not pray for until I first possessed it, I seemed tossed out helpless and forlorn into dreary darkness.

What the Bible said about God's love was altogether a secondary consideration to what I might feel about it; indeed, as far as I can recollect, I did not consider the Bible at all. "How do I feel?" not "What does God say?" was my daily cry. I was like a criminal in the presence of a judge, who, instead of being concerned as to how the judge felt about him, should spend all his efforts in trying to see how he felt about the judge.

A more ridiculous as well as pitiful attitude of soul one can hardly conceive of. And yet no one whom I approached on the subject seemed to know any better; and I floundered on in a despairing sort of way, afraid to give up my spiritual struggles lest I should be eternally damned, and yet realizing that they brought no help; and being continually tempted to upbraid God for being deaf to my cries.

I was like a man kneeling in a dark room and praying despairingly for light, ignorant of the fact that outside the sun was shining, and that it only needed to open the windows and light would pour in. In the very nature of things light, either in the physical world or the spiritual world, cannot be self-evolved. I had gone to work in entirely the wrong way. I was trying to feel before I knew; and, instead of basing my feelings upon knowledge, I was seeking to base my knowledge upon my feelings.

It was just as if a man, wanting to travel to a certain place, should enter the first railway station he might come across, and, without making any inquiries, should take a seat in the first railway carriage at hand, and should then shut his eyes and try to feel whether he was in the right train or not. No man in his senses would do such an idiotic thing. And yet it was exactly this I was doing in my religious life. It never entered my head to try and find out the facts of religion. I did not even know there were any facts to find out. My relations with God seemed to me altogether a matter of my own feelings towards Him, and not in the least of His feelings towards me; and every religious energy I possessed was consequently directed towards getting up these necessary feelings.

Of course it was an impossible task, and, as time went on, and no right feelings would come for all my striving, I became more and more discouraged, and at last, when I was between twenty-three and twenty-four, I found myself being driven into absolute unbelief. I argued that, if there really was a God anywhere, some answer to all my long and earnest wrestling would surely have been vouchsafed to me; and that, since He made no sign, therefore He could not be.

Moreover, as I grew older, I had begun to learn something more of the awful condition of things in the world because of sin; and the manifest evidences I seemed to see of an imperfect creation in my own life and in the lives of others, where failure was generally the rule, and success only the exception, appeared to me incompatible with the idea of a wise and sensible Creator, not to say a good One, such as I had been told I must believe in. And gradually the creation came to seem to me such a grievous failure that I felt driven to the conclusion that either it must have been a wicked God who had created us, or else we had not been created by God at all, but by some evil and malicious power opposed to Him.

In my diary under date of 11/5/1855, I head my entry with the following ominous words:

"The Eclipse of Faith."

"This last year has witnessed a great change in me. Every faculty of my nature has been thoroughly aroused. I have felt my mind expanding and have been cognizant of an actual and rapid mental growth. I pass from one phase of experience to another, leave behind me one standing place after another, and am now—where! Oh Christ, that I indeed knew where!

* * *

"An inevitable chain of reasoning on free will has loosened every foothold, and I know not where to rest, if indeed there *is* any rest. Without any apprehension on my part of the result, thoughts and reasonings have been slowly gathering around my faith, and dashing themselves against it, until at last, with a sudden shock, it has fallen; and I am lost!

It has come to me like this. Benevolence certainly is a necessary attribute of the Almighty. His love, we are told, surpasses the love of an earthly parent far more than we can imagine. But it is utterly inconsistent with this to suppose that He can have any foreknowledge of the destiny of the human beings He creates. For of course, did He know, His benevolence would not allow Him to create any but beings destined to eternal happiness. Therefore He cannot be omniscient. Further if He were omnipotent, as we are told, He would have made such modifications in man's nature as would at least render the work of salvation less difficult and of far more frequent occurrence. Therefore He cannot be both all loving and also all powerful. Without either of these He ceases to be a God. Either He has set in motion a creating force which He can neither control nor end, and has performed His work in the first place so imperfectly and blindly that the results are grievously disastrous; or He has nothing to do with creation, and we are created by another and an evil Power.

* * *

"A further conclusion is forced upon me. Justice is another necessary attribute of a good God. But it were most utterly unjust that we now should be feeling the effects of Adam's fall, supposing there ever was such a thing. We are driven therefore from the possibility of a just Creator making independent beings suffer eternally for each other's sins. And on the other hand benevolence could not allow of the creation of innately wicked natures, while justice could not share in punishing them.

"There is no escape! A thousand questions rush in on every side. I am a sceptic!"

CHAPTER FOURTEEN

A Renewed Search

*T*his scepticism continued for over two years, and I had quite settled down to it and looked upon it as the normal condition of every thoughtful reasonable being. But the year 1858 was destined to see everything changed. Early in that year I had become acquainted with some very orthodox Christians who were full of the doctrines and dogmas of Christianity. As I have stated before, I knew absolutely nothing of doctrines. They had never come into my scheme of religion at all. I was immensely interested therefore in hearing about them, and began to wonder whether my unbelief might not have been caused by my utter ignorance of these very doctrines. Under date of 4/25/1858, I wrote in my diary:

"The Bible talks of the necessity of being 'born again,' what *does* it mean? Is there really such a thing practically to be experienced? And is a belief in Jesus of Nazareth as the Savior of the world necessary to it? Oh, how I long for settlement. . . . It may be that all my failures to find and walk in the right way arise from my rejection of Christ in the sense in which most Christians seem to receive Him, but I really cannot receive Him so. And besides, if their way *is* the truth, I must wait until my Divine Guide leads me into it; and certainly He is not leading me there now, but, it seems to me, further and further away. . . . My whole soul and intellect seem to shrink from the material orthodox view of the Gospel. It seems impossible for me to believe in the atoning merits of Christ's death. My mind revolts from anything so material as the thought that the outward death of His body, (which after all must necessarily have taken place in some way as a consequence of His humanity), could have had any atoning merits. Far more likely, if atonement was needed at all, was it His life that was the sacrifice. To put on humanity must indeed have been to Divinity a wonderful condescension, and bitter suffering; to put it off, no matter in what way, could be none whatever.

"But I may be wrong in my views. Only the Lord can teach me."

Again on 5/18/1858, I write:

"I cannot help the feeling that I have attained to a higher form of Truth than the apostles had, and therefore I cannot pray 'Lord, I believe, help thou my unbelief' since I have no conviction of being in unbelief. I am not comfortable, however, in my belief or unbelief, whichever it may be, and yet I can see no way of escape. Last night at our Bible class I introduced the subject, hoping that my orthodox friends would be able to argue so conclusively on their side as to force me to a conviction in the orthodox form of faith. But I felt at the end that no argument could avail anything. If my belief is to be changed it will have to be by a Divine power, and it would be indeed a being 'born again.' But it seems impossible to me."

Again, on 6/25/1858, I wrote:—

"Cold and dead again and full of pride! The day will certainly come at last when it will be said of me as of Ephraim of old, 'She is wedded to her idols, let her alone!' My 'idol' now I fear is the pride of human reason which will not submit to become as a little child before it can enter the Kingdom of Heaven. . . . At present I am in great trouble because of my religious belief. I long to adopt the Orthodox creed, but cannot; and while on one hand it seems to me wicked that I cannot, at the same time it seems also wicked in me to try to do so, when a clearer light seems to have been granted me. If the truth is what the Unitarians profess, I am afraid to know it. I dread the consequences. I shrink from the contempt and reproaches it would bring upon me. And yet at the same time there is perhaps something a little pleasing to the natural human pride and heroism to think of being called upon to take an independent stand for what I consider a higher form of truth. And yet I do not want to be independent of those I love. I am in a state of sad perplexity."

This perplexity increased and deepened, and I began at last to think it was dishonest not to speak it out to my friends, and was just about making up my mind to do so, when one day an event occurred that changed the whole current of my life.

CHAPTER FIFTEEN

RESTORATION OF MY BELIEF

*I*t was in the year 1858 and I was twenty-six years old. I had just lost a precious little daughter five years old, and my heart was aching with sorrow. I could not endure to think that my darling had gone out alone into a Godless universe; and yet, no matter on which side I turned, there seemed no ray of light.

It happened that just at this time the religious world was being greatly stirred by the inauguration of daily noonday meetings, held from twelve to one, in the business part of the city, and crowded with businessmen. I had heard of these noonday meetings with a very languid interest, as I thought they were only another effort of a dying-out superstition to bolster up its cause. However, one day I happened to be near a place where one of these meetings was being held, and I thought I would go in and see what it was like. It was an impressive thing to see such crowds of busy men and women collected together at that hour in one of the busiest parts of the city, and I remember wondering vaguely what it could all be about. Then suddenly something happened to me. What it was or how it came I had no idea, but somehow an inner eye seemed to be opened in my soul, and I seemed to see that after all God was a fact—the bottom fact of all facts—and the only thing to do was to find out all about Him. It was not a pious feeling, such as I had been looking for, but it was a conviction—just such a conviction as comes to one when a mathematical problem is suddenly solved. One does not *feel* it is solved, but one knows it, and there can be no further question. I do not remember anything that was said. I do not even know that I heard anything. A tremendous revolution was going on within me that was of far profounder interest than anything the most eloquent preacher could have uttered. God was making Himself manifest as an actual existence, and my soul leaped up in an irresistible cry to know Him.

It was not that I felt myself to be a sinner needing salvation, or that I was troubled about my future destiny. It was not a personal question at all. It was simply and only that I had become aware of God, and that I felt I could not rest until I should know Him. I might be good or I might be bad; I might be going to Heaven or I might be going to hell—these things were outside the question. All I wanted was to become acquainted with the God of whom I had suddenly become aware.

How to set about it was the one absorbing question. I had no one I cared to ask, and it never occurred to me that prayer would help me. It seemed to me like the study of some new and wonderful branch of knowledge to which I must apply with all diligence, and I concluded that probably the Bible was the book I needed. "This book," I said to myself, "professes to teach us about God. I will see if it can teach me anything." I was going with my family to spend some weeks at the seashore, and I decided to take no books but the Bible, and to try and find out what it said about God. In my diary I wrote under date of 7/16/1858:

> "I have brought my Bible to Atlantic City this summer with a determination to find out what its plan of salvation is. My own plans have failed utterly, now I will try God's if possible. . . . I am trying to believe Him simply as a little child. I have laid aside my preconceived notions of what He ought to do and say, and have come in simplicity to the Bible to see what He has done and said; and I *will* believe Him."

Someone had remarked once in my hearing that the book of Romans contained the clearest and fullest statements of Christian doctrine to be found in the Bible, and I set myself to read it. What I should have made out of it without any guidance I cannot say, but one day I mentioned to a lady, who was visiting us, how interested I was in trying to understand the teaching of the Book of Romans, but how difficult I found it, when she said she had a little book which had explained it to her, and asked if she might give it to me. I accepted it eagerly, and found it most enlightening. It set forth the plan of salvation as described in the third, fourth and fifth of Romans in a clear businesslike way that appealed to me strongly. It stated that mankind were all sinners, and all deserved punishment— that all had sinned and come short of the glory of God, and that there was none righteous, no not one; and it declared that therefore every mouth was stopped and all the world had become guilty before God (Rom. 3:1-19). It went on to show that there was no escape from this except through the righteousness of Christ, which was "unto all and upon all them that believe"; and that Christ was our propitiation, through whom we obtained the "remission of sins that are past" (Rom. 3:20-26). And then it pointed out that by this process all boasting on our part was shut out, and we were justified before God, not by anything we had done or could do, but by what our Divine Savior had done for us (Rom. 3:27-31). It declared that Christ was the substitute for sinners—that He had in their place borne the punishment they deserved, and that all we had to do in order to secure the full benefit of this substitution, was simply to believe in it, and accept the forgiveness so purchased.

Of course this was a very businesslike interpretation of these passages; but I want to tell, as truthfully as I can, the way things impressed me then. The very crudeness and outwardness of the interpretation made it easy for my ignorance to grasp it, and it struck me at the time as a most sensible and satisfactory arrangement. It was a "plan of salvation" that I could understand. There was nothing mystical or mysterious about it,—no straining after emotions, no looking out for experiences. It was all the work of Another done for me, and required nothing on my part but a simple common-sense understanding and belief.

Baldly stated it was as follows. We were all sinners, and therefore all deserved punishment. But Christ had taken our sins upon Himself and had borne the punishment in our stead, and therefore an angry God was propitiated, and was willing to forgive us and let us go free. Nothing could be more plain and simple. Even a child could understand it. It was all outside of oneself, and there need be no searchings within or rakings up of one's inward feelings to make things right with God. Christ had made them right, and we had nothing to do but to accept it all as a free gift from Him. Moreover, a God who could arrange such a simple plan as this, was understandable and get-at-able, and I began to think it must be true.

This all sounds very outward and very crude; but, after all, crude as it seems, there was behind it the great bottom fact that God was, somehow or other, in Christ reconciling the world unto Himself; and it was this vital fact of the reconciliation between God and man that had laid hold of me. And I believe it is this fact, however it may be expressed, that is the one essential thing in the outset of every satisfactory religious life. The soul must know that all is right between itself and God before it can try, with any heart, to worship and serve Him.

I had discovered this vital fact, and the religious life had begun for me with eager and enthusiastic delight.

In my diary I find in 1858 the following entries:

"RESTORATION OF BELIEF."

"August 20, 1858. Am I really coming to Christ? I ask myself this question with wonder and amazement. A month ago it seemed so utterly impossible. But I believe I am. It seems as if these truths in the New Testament have taken hold of my soul, and I cannot gainsay them. God only knows what the end will be.

"August 21, 1858. Many passages of Scripture have been impressed on my mind in my reading, and, having made up my mind simply to believe and not to reason or question, I *do* find myself inevitably brought to Christ as my Redeemer. My watchword for the last few weeks has been 'Thus saith the Lord' as a conclusive argument in every case.

"August 30,1858. I am resting now simply on God's own record as the foundation of my hope. He says Jesus Christ is His well-beloved Son, and I believe it. He says further that He gave His Son to be the propitiation for our sins, and I believe this also. He *is* my Savior, not only my helper; and in His finished work I rest. Even my hard heart of unbelief can no longer refrain from crying out 'Lord, I believe. Help Thou my unbelief.'

"September 13, 1858. My heart is filled with the exceeding preciousness of Christ. And I am lost in wonder at the realization of His infinite mercy to me, who am so utterly unworthy of the least favor from His hands. How could He be so tender and so loving! I can write the words, 'It is all of free grace,' but they only feebly convey the deep sense I have of the infinite freeness of this grace. 'While we were yet sinners Christ died for us.' Could anything be more free than this? I have so long bewildered myself with trying to work out my own righteousness, and have found such weariness in it, that I feel as if I could never appreciate deeply enough the blessed rest there is for me in Christ. 'He was made sin for us who knew no sin, that we might be made the righteousness of God in Him.' No wonder the Apostle cried out from a full heart, 'Thanks be unto God for His unspeakable gift!'"

My diary is full of similar records, but these will suffice to tell of the wonderful discovery I had made. I want it to be clearly understood that it all came to me as a discovery, and in no sense as an attainment. I had been seeking after attainments in the past, but now I had lost all thought of any attainment of my own in the blaze of my discoveries of the salvation through Christ. It was no longer in the slightest degree a question of what I was or what I could do, but altogether a question of what God was and of what He had done. I seemed to have left myself, as myself, out of it entirely, and to care only to find out all I could about the work of Christ.

The thing that amazed me was how I could have lived so long in a world that contained the Bible, and never have found all this before. Why had nobody ever told me? How could people, who had found it out, have kept such a marvelous piece of good news to themselves? Certainly I could not keep it to myself, and I determined that no one whom I could reach should be left a day longer in ignorance, as far as I could help it. I began to buttonhole everybody, pulling them into corners and behind doors to tell them of the wonderful and delightful things I had discovered in the Bible about the salvation through the Lord Jesus Christ. It seemed to me the most magnificent piece of good news that any human being had ever had to tell, and I gloried in telling it.

So little however had I known of Christian ideas and Christian nomenclature, that I had not the least conception that what I had discovered made any difference in me personally, or that my belief in all this made me what they called a Christian. It only seemed to me that I had found out something delightful about God, which had filled me with happiness, and which I wanted everybody else to know. But that this discovery constituted what was called "conversion," or that I personally was different in any way from what I had been before, never entered my head.

One day, however, a "Plymouth Brother" friend, hearing me tell my story, exclaimed "Thank God, Mrs. Smith, that you have at last become a Christian." So little did I understand him, that I promptly replied, "Oh, no, I am not a Christian at all. I have only found out a wonderful piece of good news that I never knew before." "But," he persisted, "that very discovery makes you a Christian, for the Bible says that whoever believes this good news has passed from death unto life, and is born of God. *You* have just said that you believe it and rejoice in it, so of course *you* have passed from death unto life and are born of God." I thought for a moment, and I saw the logic of what he said. There was no escaping it. And with a sort of gasp I said, "Why, so I must be. Of course I believe this good news, and therefore of course I must be born of God. Well, I *am* glad."

From that moment the matter was settled, and not a doubt as to my being a child of God and the possessor of eternal life, has ever had the slightest power over me since. I rushed to my Bible to make myself sure there was no mistake, and I found it brimming over with this teaching. "He that believeth *hath*," "He that believeth *is*." There seemed to be nothing more to be said about it. Three passages especially struck me. First John 5:1, "Whosoever believeth that Jesus is the Christ is born of God;" and John 3:24, "Verily, verily I say unto you, He that heareth My word and believeth on Him that sent Me, hath everlasting life, and shall not come into condemnation, but is passed from death unto life"; and above all, John 20:30, 31, "And many other signs truly did Jesus in the presence of His disciples, which are not written in this book: but these are written, that ye might believe that Jesus is the Christ, the Son of God; and that, believing, ye might have life through His name."

There seemed nothing more to be said. There were things about Christ, written in the Bible, as clear as daylight, and I believed what was written with all my heart and soul, and therefore I could not doubt that I was one of those who had "life through His name." The question was settled without any further argument. It had nothing to do with how I felt, but only with what God had said. The logic seemed to me irresistible; and it not only convinced me then, but it has carried me triumphantly through every form of doubt as to my relations with God which has ever assailed me since. And I can recommend it as an infallible receipt to every doubter.

Of course at once, on having made this further discovery, of the fact that I was a Christian, I began to add it to the story I had already been telling, always ending my recital with the words—"And now, if you believe all this, you are a Christian, for the Bible says that he that believeth *is* born of God, and *has* eternal life."

I had got hold of that which is the necessary foundation of all religion, namely reconciliation with God, and had had my first glimpse of Him as He is revealed in the face of Jesus Christ. All my fear of Him had vanished. He loved me, He forgave me, He was on my side, and all was right between us. I had learned moreover that it was from the life and words of Christ that my knowledge of God was to come, and not, as I had always thought, from my own inward feelings; and my relief was inexpressible.

I can see now, in looking back, that in many respects I had only touched the surface of the spiritual realities hidden under the doctrines I had so eagerly embraced. I was as yet only in the beginning of things. But it was a beginning in the right direction, and was the introduction to the "life more abundant" which, as my story will show, was to come later. Meanwhile I had got my first glimpse of the unselfishness of God. As yet it was only a glimpse, but it was enough to make me radiantly happy.

CHAPTER SIXTEEN

THE ASSURANCE
OF FAITH

I was so filled with enthusiasm over my discovery, that nothing else seemed to me of the slightest importance; and, as I have said, I attacked every friend I had on the subject, and insisted on knowing whether they too had found out the transcendent fact that their sins were all forgiven, and that they were the children of God. I simply *compelled* them to listen, whether they wanted to or not, for it seemed to me the most pitiful thing conceivable that anybody should fail to know it, while I was alive to tell it. And I must say that nearly every one I spoke to, partly perhaps because of their surprise at being attacked so vigorously, listened with eager interest, and sooner or later embraced the views I so enthusiastically declared. Very many of my friends of course really were already Christians, but had hardly dared to think themselves so; and to them my teaching brought the assurance of faith they so sorely needed.

In fact it seemed to me such a wonderful bit of good news, that I thought if I would go into the street and stand at the corners, and begin to tell it, everybody would open the doors and windows to listen to my story. I felt like a herald marching through the corridors of a prison, with a proclamation from the King, of free pardon to every prisoner. Paul's message in the Synagogue of the Jews at Antioch, when he spoke to them about Jesus, and said, "Be it known unto you therefore, men and brethren, that through this man is preached unto you the forgiveness of sins; and by Him all that believe are justified from all things from which ye could not be justified by the law of Moses," was my message; and the marvel to me was that every prisoner did not at once, on hearing it, open the door of his cell and walk out a free man. It seemed to me superlatively silly for any one, in the face of such a proclamation, to hesitate a single moment. Why should they worry about their sins, when God had so plainly declared that Christ had borne their sins in "His own body on the tree," and had taken them away forever? Why should they fear God's anger, when the Bible had assured us that "God was in Christ reconciling the world unto Himself, not imputing their trespasses unto them"? All these wretched doubts and fears seemed then, and have always seemed since, not only irreligious and a libel against the trustworthiness of God, but also as an evidence of a great lack of good sense. Either God is true, or He is a liar. If I believe He is true, then good sense demands that I should accept His statements as the statements of facts, and should rest in them as facts.

One of the most helpful things to me at this time was a tract called "The Fox Hunter" by Caesar Malan. It was the clearest and most logical presentation of justification by faith that I have ever come across, and it proved to me beyond the possibility of question that the "assurance of faith" was at once the only biblical ground anyone could take, and also the only commonsense ground as well. The foxes in this tract were doubts, and the hunter was the preacher who caught and killed them. And its whole teaching was, that if God *said* Christ had taken away our sins, then He certainly had done so, and they were of course gone, and it was not only folly but also presumption in us not to believe it.

I continually asked myself why every preacher did not tell out these facts clearly and fully so that no one could fail to understand them? And I felt this so strongly that, whenever I heard sermons that seemed to leave the matter uncertain, or confused, I thought nothing of going up to the preachers afterwards and expostulating with them, because they had not clearly preached the Gospel of Christ. I am convinced, in looking back now, that I must have made myself a general nuisance to our dear Quaker preachers, whose preaching I confess was not often in those days of this definite sort; but the truth was that what I had discovered seemed to me of such paramount and overwhelming importance, that no other consideration was worth a moment's notice. I felt compelled to tell it to every one I could reach. The dear quiet Friends could not understand such excessive, and, I dare say, unwise zeal, and my visits at any of their houses were fairly dreaded. Even my brothers-in-law were almost afraid to have me visit my own sisters, and in many ways I went through a sort of persecution, which no doubt I largely brought upon myself by my unadvised zeal, but which at the time seemed to me a martyrdom for the truth.

It is not often, I think that the story of the Gospel comes so vividly to any one as it did to me. But from the fact that, as a Quaker, I had no doctrinal teaching, all that I was learning about the salvation in Christ came in a perfect blaze of illumination. The Bible seemed fairly radiant with the "glad tidings of great joy," and I wondered every one did not see it. As I knew literally nothing of theology, and had never heard any theological terms, I took the whole Gospel story in the most commonsense way possible, and believed it without any reservations. I often said I was like a prisoner who had come out of a dark underground cell into the light of ten thousand suns. And in spite of all the disapproval and opposition of the Elders and Overseers among the Quakers, and of my own family as well, my enthusiasm gained me a hearing, and nearly every friend I had came, sooner or later, into a knowledge of the truths I advocated, and more or less shared my rejoicing; so that gradually the opposition died down, and in the end, while the "solid Friends" could not fully endorse me, they at least left me free to continue my course unmolested.

No doubt the crudeness of my views was very patent to the more advanced spiritual Christians around me, and I feel sure now that a large part of the opposition I met with arose from this fact. But while I might wish my views had been more mature, I can never regret the enthusiasm that made me so eager to tell out to everyone the best I knew.

And even the opposition was blessed to me, for it taught me some most invaluable lessons. I came across a book in those days, the name of which I regret to say I have forgotten, which helped me enormously. Its central thought was that one of the richest gifts a Christian could have was the gift of persecution, and that to be like the Master in being rejected of men, was the highest dignity to which a Christian could attain. It taught that he was the greatest

Christian who was willing to take the lowest place, and that to become the chief of all could only be attained by becoming the servant of all. I was so impressed by this teaching that I tried to put it in practice; and, whenever I expected in any interview to meet with reproof or opposition, I would always beforehand pray fervently that I might receive it in a true Christian spirit. I was much helped, too, by a saying of Madame Guyon's, that she had learned to be thankful for every snub and mortification, because she had found that they helped to advance her in the spiritual life; and in time I learned something of the same lesson.

The especial advantage I gained from the disapproval I met with was that it took a great deal of the conceit out of me. I had it so rubbed into me that I was altogether wrong and foolish, and was only tolerated because of the kindness of my friends, that I really came at last to have a sort of instinctive feeling that I deserved nothing but snubs and reproaches, and that any unkindness that might be shown me was only my just desert. In fact I got into the habit of never expecting anything else, and ceased to think I had any rights that others ought not to trample on. This habit of mind has given me the greatest liberty of spirit through all my life since, as I have never been obliged, as so many people seem to be, to stand up for my rights, and have in fact scarcely ever had the sense to see when I have been slighted. If one has no rights, their rights cannot be trampled on, and if one has no feelings, their feelings cannot be hurt. So deeply was this lesson engraved upon my soul by what I went through at the time of which I am speaking, that to this day I am always surprised at any kindness that is shown me, as at something entirely unexpected and undeserved. I do not know any lesson I have ever learned that has been so practically helpful as this lesson, learned from the opposition I met with in the early years of my Christian experience; although I have no doubt, as I have said, that I brought my trials largely upon myself, by my crudeness and my ignorance.

Crude and ignorant as I was, I had however, as I have said, got a firm grip on one magnificent foundation truth that nothing has ever been able to shake, and this was that God was in Christ reconciling the world unto Himself, not imputing their trespasses unto them. All was right between my soul and God. He was my Father, and I was His child, and I had nothing to fear. It was no matter that I had got hold of it in a crude sort of way. The thing was that I *had* got hold of it. There it was—the grand central fact of God's love and God's forgiveness, and my soul was at rest about this forever.

CHAPTER SEVENTEEN

MY LIFE OF FAITH

*T*he disapproval of my own religious society, in these early stages of my new life, threw me very much under the influence of the Plymouth Brethren, who were at that time making quite a stir in Philadelphia, and whose clear teaching of doctrines, and especially of the doctrine of "justification by faith," was particularly congenial to my new way of looking at things. They were great Bible students, and I soon found under their teaching a fascinating interest in Bible study. It was all new ground to me, and I went into it with the greatest avidity. So delighted was I with the treasures I found in its pages, that at first my one fear was lest, as the Bible was such a short book, I should soon exhaust it, and come to the end of its delights, and I used to stint myself to small portions in order to spin it out the longer. But I soon found that this was not at all necessary, as the more I studied, the more I found there was to study, and each passage seemed to have a thousand continually unfolding meanings. The book was no larger than I thought, but it was infinitely deeper. It seemed to me something as if the truths in the Bible were covered with a multitude of skins, and as if, as I studied, one skin after another was peeled off, leaving the words the same, but the meaning of those words deeper and higher. I can never be thankful enough to the Plymouth Brethren for introducing me to the fascinations of Bible study.

It was a wonderful and delightful life I had now begun to live. I had begun to know God, and I was finding Him to be lovely and lovable beyond my fondest imaginings. The romance of my life had dawned. I cannot say how religion may have affected other people, but to me my religion has been all through a fascinating and ever-unfolding romance. If for nothing else, I pity the poor unfortunate Agnostics of the present day for their missing of this most delightful of all romances. They can have nothing I am sure in all their lives to equal it. The nearest approach that I can think of to a like experience is the delight of exploring an unknown science, or a new field of mental research; but even that cannot equal, I am sure, the delights of exploring the Science of God. Imagine it for a moment. To have got on the track of a real acquaintance with the ways and character of God, the Creator of heaven and earth, and to be making continually fresh discoveries of new and delightful things about Him—what scientific research could be as entrancing? All that I had longed for and agonized over in my first awakening, was coming to me in clearest vision, day by day, and the ever-recurring delight of new revelations and new ideas was more delicious than words could express. Then too the joy of telling it all to others, and the enormous satisfaction of seeing their faces lighten, and their hearts expand, as their souls made the same discoveries as my own. Ah, no one who has not experienced it, can know the fascination of it all!

I do not mean to say that I discovered everything at once, nor even that all I thought I had discovered proved to be permanent truth. My story, as I continue, will show that this was not the case. Like all novices in scientific research, I grasped many half-truths, and came to many false conclusions. But the search of itself was delicious, and the finding out of one's mistakes far surpassed the mortification at having made them.

My soul had started on its voyage of discovery, and to become acquainted with God was its unalterable and unceasing aim. I was as yet only at the beginning, but what a magnificent beginning it was. God was a reality, and He was my God. He had created me, and He loved me, and all was right between us. All care about my own future destiny had been removed from my shoulders. I could say with Paul, "I know whom I have believed, and am persuaded that He is able to keep that which I have committed unto Him against that day." I needed no longer to work *for* my soul's salvation, but only to work *out* the salvation that had been bestowed upon me. All the years of my self-introversion and self-examination were ended. Instead of my old fruitless searchings into my feelings and emotions for some tangible evidence of God's favor, the glorious news, declared in the Bible, that He so loved the world as to have sent His only begotten Son to save the world, absorbed every faculty.

It was no longer "How do I feel?" but always "What does God say?" And He said such delightful things, that to find them out became my supreme delight. I do not mean what He said to me personally in my heart, but what He had said to every human being in the Bible—the good news of salvation in the Lord Jesus Christ. Anything said to myself alone might be open to doubt, as to whether it was really myself who was meant, but anything said to the whole world could not help including me, and I greedily appropriated it all.

This went on for several years, during which I had a really glorious time. Between the joys of discovery on the one hand, and the joys of telling others about my discoveries on the other, my cup of the wine of life was full and overflowing. I had plenty of earthly trials, but somehow they were in the background compared to the fascinations of my religious life. Nothing that belonged only to the earthly life could really matter, when one's soul was daily tasting the blissful joy of reconciliation with God, and of being made a partaker of the glorious salvation of the Lord Jesus Christ.

It was in the year 1865 that the most fascinating of all the epochs in my spiritual romance dawned upon my soul.

I had been a Christian nine years, and had had, as I have said, a delightful and enchanting time; but what was coming now was so far ahead of all that was past, that it seemed as if a new and magical world had opened before me.

My religion during those nine years had been perfectly satisfactory as far as God was concerned, and the discoveries I had made of His ways and His character had been all of them most delightful. But on my own side the satisfaction was much less complete. I was very happy, but I was not as good as I wanted to be. I had found a religion that provided perfectly for my future deliverance, but it did not seem to give me present deliverance. I had found an unselfish and a just God, whom I could worship and adore, without any fear of being disappointed; but I was continually disappointed in myself.

I knew I was not what I ought to be. My life was full of failure and sin. Not outward sins so much, as sins of the heart, coldness, deadness, want of Christian love, roots of bitterness,—all those inward sins over which the children of God so often seem to mourn. When I would do good evil was present with me, and the good that I would I did not, while the evil that I would not that I did. I was continually sinning and repenting, making good resolutions and breaking them, hating what was wrong, and yet yielding to it, longing for victory, and sometimes getting it, but more often failing.

I could not help, however, seeing all the while that the Bible seemed to imply that Christ came to bring a real and present victory to His followers, and that it was intended that Christians should be delivered from their anxious cares and fears, and were to enjoy now and here a peace that passed all understanding. But I was painfully conscious that I knew very little of this. My soul it is true was at rest as to my future, but in the present it was racked and torn by a thousand daily cares and anxieties. The very fruits of that Spirit, which as a Christian, I believed I had received, were love, joy, peace, long-suffering, gentleness, meekness, goodness, and these were just the very things in which I knew myself to be the most deficient.

This was not what I had expected when I first became a Christian. From the peaceful, restful lives of the Quakers, among whom I had been brought up, and from their teaching of the paramount and vital necessity of being good, I had supposed of course that becoming a Christian meant necessarily becoming peaceful and good, and I had as much expected to have victory over sin and over worries as I had expected the sun to shine. But I was forced to confess in the secret depths of my soul that I had been disappointed.

At first, it is true, the joys of my new-found salvation had carried me triumphantly over everything, and I had thought that temptation, and sin, and worry, and fear, had all been swept away forever. But in a little while, when the first glow had passed away, I found the old temptations coming back with all their old power, and it became just as easy as ever to be anxious, and worried, and care-burdened, and irritable, and unkind, and critical, and severe, and in short to do and to be all the ugly things from which I had expected religion to deliver me. This did not for a moment shake my faith in the fact that I was a child of God and an heir of Heaven, but it often made me feel very mean, and very much ashamed of myself. To be a child of God, and yet to be unable to act like one, made me wonder whether I could have missed something in religion which would have given me victory, and I determined to find out if possible what that something was. I questioned several older Christians about it, but from one and all I received the same answer. "No," they said, "you have not missed anything. The life of sinning and repenting is all we can expect in this world, because of the weakness of the flesh." They explained to me that there were two natures in us—the old Adam which was ours at our natural birth, and the new Adam which became ours when we were born again by the Spirit of God, and that these two natures were always warring against each other, sometimes one getting the victory and sometimes the other, and that only in death should we know any real delivery from the old Adam.

Nothing could have described my condition better than the Apostle's account of his own condition in Rom. 7:14-23. It seemed as if it might have been written for me, and continually I cried out with him, "Oh wretched man that I am! who shall deliver me from the body of this death?" But I could not help wondering why Paul could ever have asked that question, since he must surely have known that in this life there was no such deliverance to be found. He certainly was aware, I reasoned, that the "body of death," or the "old man," under which he groaned, was always to dwell within him and fetter him, and that, until death should release him from its hateful presence, he need not look for any release. And yet continually the fact stared me in the face, that Paul had not only asked that question, but had also answered it, as though he really believed there was a way of deliverance, and had said triumphantly, "I thank God through Jesus Christ our Lord." But what I asked myself, could he have meant by this triumphant reply? I had entered into the salvation through Jesus Christ our Lord, and yet I knew no such triumphant deliverance from the "body of death" within me, but was continually brought into bondage to it. Why was it? Where was the difficulty?

This feeling became especially strong after my discovery of the unlimited love of God. It seemed such an ungenerous return to His boundless unselfishness to be so lacking in those fruits of the Spirit, which the Bible showed us He looked for from His people, that my whole soul cried out against it. Moreover, since He had shown Himself to be so mighty to save in the future, how could I believe He was so powerless in the present.

The Quaker examples and influences around me seemed to say there must a deliverance somewhere, for they declared that they had experienced it; although they never seemed able to explain the "what" or the "how" in such a manner as that I could understand it.

There was also another influence in my life that seemed to tell the same story. I possessed a book which distinctly taught that God's children were not only commanded to bring forth the fruits of the Spirit, but also that they could do so; and which seemed to reveal the mystical pathway towards it. It was called "Spiritual Progress," and was a collection of extracts from the writings of Fenelon and Madame Guyon. This book was very dear to me, for it had been a gift from my adored father, and always lay on my desk beside my Bible. When my father was quite a young man, in fact only eighteen years old, he was one day walking along the streets of Philadelphia on his way to join his ship for a long voyage to China, and, passing a second-hand book stall, the thought occurred to him to purchase a book to read during his voyage. He had but lately entered into the spiritual life, and was attracted by the title of an old book called "Spiritual Progress," for sale for a few pence. He knew nothing of the book, but bought it at a venture, as far as his own consciousness was concerned, but unconsciously no doubt guided by the Lord whom he had begun to trust. He says in his Reminiscences—"This book proved to be of the greatest comfort to me. I carried it in my pocket, and at leisure moments read it to my everlasting profit, I trust. And I cannot but thank a kind Providence for giving me this blessed book."

He valued the book so highly that, as fast as his children grew old enough, he presented each one of us with a copy, and asked us to read it carefully. Our father was so dear to us that we always wanted to please him, and I for one had made the book my special companion during all the time of my first hungry and hopeless search after God. Being a book intended to teach souls how to progress in the spiritual life, rather than how to enter into that life, it was not of much definite help to me in those days of my blind searching; and when in 1858 I came into the knowledge of what I believed to be "the plan of salvation" settled upon in the councils of Heaven, and revealed to us in the life and death of Christ, and formulated and tabulated by the Apostle Paul, I filled the margins of my copy of the book with what I felt to be unanswerable criticisms as to its unsoundness.

But all unconsciously to myself its teachings had made a profound impression upon me; and, even while I criticized, I still was often conscious of an underlying hunger after the mystical side of religion set forth in this book. And, during all the years that followed, I was more or less tossed to and fro between the claims of Plymouth Brethrenism on one side and the claims of mysticism on the other. The practical business part of my nature inclined me to the former, while my Quaker inheritance and bringing up, and the influence of my book inclined me to the latter. At one time I would think doctrines were of the first importance, and life comparatively insignificant, and at other times doctrines would seem to be worthless, unless backed by and resulting in a righteous life. Sometimes Paul would have the ascendancy, with his teaching of salvation by faith, and sometimes James, with his teaching that faith without works was dead. My Plymouth Brethren friends exalted Paul, with his justification by faith, my dear Quaker friends and the Catholic Saints of my book exalted James with his justification by works. The business faculty in me leaned to the first, but the mystic side of my nature leaned to the last. The result was an intermittent unrest of soul, which, combined with my distress at my many failures, often made me question, as I have said, whether what I had learned of the salvation of Christ could really be all that that salvation had to offer.

Not knowing what else to do, I turned more and more to "sound doctrines" to quiet my unrest. Under Plymouth Brethren influence these had become very clearly defined; and they were all duly ticketed and safely deposited in the cubby-holes of my mind, each doctrine in its own recess, with its name clearly marked underneath. Nothing could have been neater or more orderly, as far as doctrines were concerned. And I had become quite a successful teacher of these same doctrines, and looked down pityingly upon everybody who was less clear and definite than myself. I often used to wish I could have most of the religious teachers I knew seated in a row on baby high chairs before me, that I might explain to them the doctrines they seemed to be so confused about, especially the doctrines of "justification by faith" and the "judicial standing of the believer." I often declared that if you only had these two points clearly defined, and believed in them fully, you were all right, and need not trouble about much else.

I remember saying something of this kind to a cousin who had come to me, troubled about her shortcomings in the Christian life, and she exclaimed, "Why, Hannah, according to what you say, all our sins, past, present, and to come, are forgiven, if we only

believe, and it really makes very little difference what we do."
"Yes," I said, in my ignorance, "that is just the beauty of it. We are
clothed with the robe of Christ's righteousness, and that robe covers
up all the vileness that is underneath, and when God looks at us He
sees, not our unrighteousness, but the righteousness of Christ, and
accepts us because of that."

Another time a good Quaker Preacher, who had heard me ex-
pounding these crude views said, "It seems to me, Hannah Smith,
that thou talks as if thou could go to a ready-made clothing shop,
and buy garments of salvation, and put them on then and there, and
come out clothed with righteousness and ready for heaven." "Yes,"
I said, "that is just how it is, only I do not need to buy the garments, they are given to me by Christ. Thank thee for such a beautiful illustration, I shall certainly use it to preach from."

I have no doubt I took the Plymouth Brethren teaching in a far
more outward and literal sense than was ever intended by them, but
I always liked to define things clearly to my own mind, and this
seemed to me the logical outcome of their teaching. Strangely
enough, I failed to see the incongruity of a God of righteousness
covering up our unrighteousness with the robe of His own righteousness, and then making believe to Himself that we were fit for
heaven, when all the while He must know perfectly well that it was
nothing but an outward show, and that, underneath His beautiful
robe, our own "filthy garments" were still upon us. When now and
then this was suggested to me by some of my Quaker friends, I sti-
fled the misgivings their suggestions awakened, by saying to myself, that, although they were dear, good people, they were not at
all doctrinal, and knew very little about the "plan of salvation" or
"justification by faith," or the "judicial standing of the believer,"
and that their opinions, therefore, were not worth considering.

After, however, the discovery I had made of the wideness of
God's love, as described in my last chapters, I began to feel more
and more uneasy. It seemed to me a most ungrateful return for such
boundless love, that we, who were the objects of it, should fail so
lamentably in living the sort of life which we could not but plainly
see was the life He intended we should live. And more and more I
felt the inconsistency of having a salvation, which was in the end to
be so magnificently complete, but which failed now and here so
conspicuously in giving that victory over sin and over worry, that
seemed everywhere in the gospel to be set forth as the present result
of this salvation.

Why was it, I asked myself over and over, that the God, who had planned such a glorious deliverance for us in the future, had not also planned a better deliverance in the present?

CHAPTER EIGHTEEN

THE WAY OF ESCAPE

*T*his unrest and questioning came to a culmination in the year 1865. Family circumstances had in that year made it necessary for us to leave our delightful home in Germantown, and all our wide interests there, to live in a remote village in New Jersey, where we were almost entirely isolated from any congenial society. It was a pecuniary advantage to us, but was otherwise a very great trial, to me especially, and I confess that my spirit rebelled sorely at the change.

Little did I dream that it was here, in this very place, which seemed to me so isolated and desolate, that a glorious light was to dawn, and the fourth and crowning epoch of my religious life was to be ushered in.

It came about in this wise. I was, as I have said, very rebellious at my change of abode and surroundings. But I had enough spiritual insight to know that this rebellion was wrong; that, since the change was a providential arrangement over which I had no control, the only right thing for me to do was to accept it cheerfully, and to say heartily, "Thy will be done," in regard to it. But although I scolded myself about it continually, I did not seem able to bring myself to the point of accepting God's will; and as a fact I did not really want to accept it. I felt that it was very hard lines for me to be obliged to leave my happy home in Germantown, and my sphere of usefulness there, to live in such a lonely far off place as Millville; and it seemed to me that God ought not to have allowed it, and that I had a right to grumble and fret. As a consequence I got into a most uncomfortable state of mind where even my clear doctrines failed to help me, and I began at last to be afraid that I was going to lose every bit of religion I possessed.

In the face of a real need such as this, it was no satisfaction to know I was forgiven. I wanted more than forgiveness, I wanted deliverance. But how to get deliverance I could not conceive.

As we had a good many Mission preachers visiting us from time to time, I laid my case before several of them, and asked for help, but no one seemed able to tell me anything. Finally a very successful religious teacher came for a few days, and to him I poured out my trouble very fully, and begged him to suggest some way of deliverance. He took my case into serious consideration, and said he believed that what I needed was to undertake some Christian work, and that if I would start out the next morning and visit the poor people in the neighborhood, and see what I could do to help them, he thought I would find my spiritual life renewed, and all would be right. Accordingly the next day I proceeded to try the proposed remedy. But it did not take me long to find out what a futile remedy it was. In almost the first house I entered, I found a woman in the same sort of difficulty as my own, and sorely needing help, and I had no help to give. It seemed to me I was like a person trying to feed hungry people out of an empty bowl, and I saw that this was a silly and impossible thing to do. I went home more discouraged than ever, convinced, that, before I could help any one else, I must find some deliverance for myself.

There was a little dressmaker in the village who often came to sew for me; and, having so little society in the neighborhood, I would sometimes sit down and talk with her, as we sewed together. She seemed an unusually spiritually minded Christian, and I was much interested in her experiences. I found out that she held the view that there really was such a thing as victory over temptation, and that it was not necessary, as I had thought, to go on all your life sinning and repenting, but that a Christian might actually be delivered. She told me that among the Methodists there was a doctrine taught which they called the "Doctrine of Holiness," and that there was an experience called "sanctification" or the "second blessing" which brought you into a place of victory. I was immensely interested in all she had to say about it, and began to hope that perhaps I might here find the solution of my difficulties.

She told me there was a little meeting held in the village on Saturday evenings, where this doctrine was taught, and where people gave their experiences in regard to it, and urged me to attend it. I thought I might go some time, but I allowed things to interfere, feeling convinced that poor ignorant factory people could not have much to teach me. I had studied and taught the Bible a great deal, and had rather a high idea of my own religious attainments in that direction, and I felt that, if I should go to the meeting, I should probably have much more to teach them than they could possibly have to teach me.

At last, however, one evening, I made up my mind to give them the favor of my presence, and I confess a great favor I felt it to be. I went to the meeting, therefore, full of my own importance and my own superiority, and thought it very likely that I should astonish them by my great biblical knowledge. When I entered the meeting, a factory woman with a shawl over her head (she probably did not possess a bonnet), was speaking, and I heard her say these words: "My whole horizon used to be filled with this great big *Me* of mine, but when I got a sight of Christ as my perfect Savior, this great big *Me* wilted down to nothing."

These words were a revelation to me. I realized that I knew nothing whatever of any such experience. My *"Me"* was very big and very self-assertive, and I could not imagine how it could, by any possibility, "wilt down into nothing." But a profound conviction came to me that this must be real Christianity, and that it was, perhaps, the very thing I was longing for. Needless to say, I did not undertake to do any teaching that night, but sat as a learner at the feet of these humble Christians, who knew but little of book learning, but whose souls were evidently taught by the Holy Spirit depths of spiritual truth of which I understood nothing. I began to attend the meeting regularly as a learner, and to embrace every opportunity possible to talk with those who understood this life. I found that the gist of it was exactly what Paul meant when he said, "Not I, but Christ," and that the victory I sought, was to come by ceasing to live my own life, and by letting the power of God "work in me to will and to do of His good pleasure."

In my diary under date of 10/18/1866, I say:

183

"The Lord has been teaching me in many ways of late my utter weakness in the presence of temptation. I have grown much in knowledge, but I have not grown in grace, and I find that I have not actually any more power over sin than I had when I was first converted. This has not caused me to doubt the fact of my being a child of God, justified and forgiven, a possessor of eternal life and an heir of a heavenly inheritance. But, even while having this assurance, and never losing it, I have found that, while my heart condemns me, I cannot be happy; and I have been led to long for more holiness, for more power over sin, for more uninterrupted communion with God. But how to get at it I could not tell. Resolutions have proved utterly useless, and my own efforts have been all in vain. My prayers have been unanswered; and I have been ready a thousand times to give up in despair, and to conclude that it was not the will of God that I should ever attain to a victory over sin. And yet the Bible presents such a different picture of the Christian life,—'blameless, harmless, without rebuke,' with every temptation a 'way of escape,' 'purified,' 'conformed to the image of Christ,' 'holy as He is holy.'

"I find there are some Christians who say that by receiving Christ by faith for our sanctification, just as we received Him by faith for our justification, all this work that I long for is accomplished. That is, the *way* of accomplishing it is discovered. It is found out that the Bible teaches that the Lord can deliver from the power of sin as well as from its guilt, and the soul learns to trust Him to do it, and ceases to rely upon its own resolutions, or upon its own efforts after holiness, but commits the whole work of being kept from evil and delivered from temptation, to the Lord alone.

"I begin to see more clearly that the Lord is worthy of my most unlimited and boundless confidence; and perhaps this is the dawning of the light I have been groping for.

"It is a Methodist doctrine, and I have been used to hearing Methodists much objected to on account of it, but it seems to be the only thing that can supply *my* needs, and I feel impelled to try it."

Under date of 2/11/1867, I record my efforts to lay hold of this conquering faith, and add:

"The present attitude of my soul is that of trusting in the Lord. And I have found it is a practical reality that He *does* deliver. When temptation comes, if I turn at once to Him, breathing this prayer, 'Lord, save me. I cannot save myself from this sin, but Thou canst and wilt,' He never fails me. Either He completely changes my feelings in the case, or He causes me to forget all about it, and my victory, or rather *His* victory, is entire. This is a secret of the Christian life that I never knew before. . . . But why have I not known it? Why has my course been such a halting, miserable one, when I might have lived in victory? What striking proof I have been of the inherent legality and unbelief of the human heart, for, while trusting the Lord entirely and only for my justification, I have always been trusting myself for my sanctification. . . . I have depended upon my own efforts, my own resolutions, my own watchfulness, my own fervency, my own strivings, to accomplish the work of holy living. This was legality. It was as truly legality as if I had trusted to these things to save my soul in the first place. I was 'frustrating' the grace of God as really in regard to my sanctification as those whom I have been used to condemn so utterly as legalists, were doing it in regard to their justification. I could easily see how they made the death of Christ of none effect by their legal strivings, but I was blind to the fact that I also was doing the same thing. Our strivings to be sure were with a different end in view, but it was still in both cases our own striving—in both it was self, and not Christ. 'For, if righteousness come by the law, then Christ is dead in vain.' But now how different it is! Now I commit my daily life to Him, as well as my future destiny, and I trust Him just as nakedly for the one as for the other. I am equally powerless in both cases. I can do nothing—not even I, the new man—and if the Lord does not do it all, it will not be done. But oh! glorious truth, He *does* do it! When I trust Him He gives me deliverance from the power of sin as well as from its guilt. I can leave all in His care—my cares, my temptations, my growth, my service, my daily life moment by moment. Oh the rest and calm of a life like this.

". . . And this is the Methodist 'blessing of holiness.' Couched by them it is true in terms that I cannot altogether endorse, and held amid what seems to me a mixture of error, but still really and livingly experienced and enjoyed by them.

I feel truly thankful to them for their testimony to its reality, and I realize that it is far better to *have* the experience, even if mixed with error, than to live without it, and be very doctrinally correct, as was my former case."

My diary at this date is full of the wonderful discoveries I was making, but these extracts will suffice. From this time the possibilities of faith opened out before me in a way I had never dreamed of. I saw that it was in very truth the victory that overcometh the world, and I marveled at my blindness in never having discovered it before. For a third time a skin seemed to be peeled off the Bible, and it became again a new book to me.

> "The truth that was mine yesterday
>   Is larger truth to-day;
> Its face has aspect more divine
>   Its kingship fuller sway.
> For truth must grow, as ages roll,
> And God looms larger in the soul."

One day I was present at a meeting where the speaker read John 15, and the words "Without Me ye can do nothing" struck me with amazement. Hundreds of times before I had read and repeated these words, and had even preached from them. But now, so ablaze were they with wondrous meaning, that it almost seemed as if they must have been newly inserted in the Bible since last I had opened it. Here was our Lord saying distinctly, "Without Me ye can do nothing," and yet all the while I had been thinking I could and I must do so much! What sort of meaning had I been giving hitherto to this word "nothing"? I tried to remember, but all was a blank. I simply had not even noticed it.

Another day I came across in my reading that passage in the sixth of Matthew, where our Lord exhorts us to "take no thought for our life," on the ground that our Heavenly Father takes thought for us; and bases His assertion on the fact that, since God cares for the fowls of the air and the lilies of the field, He must necessarily do at least as much for His children who are, He Himself declares, of more value than many sparrows. I read the passage over and over with utter amazement. Could it really be true? Had it actually been in the Bible all these years? And, if it had, why had I never seen it? And yet as a fact not only had I seen it, but I had even known it by heart, and had many times repeated it. But in the only sense worth considering I never had seen it before. Now I saw; and, at the sight, cares, and worries, and fears, and anxieties, vanished like mists before the sun.

And it was the same with all the old familiar texts—they were literally illuminated with a new meaning. Every page of the Bible seemed to declare in trumpet tones the reality of a victorious and triumphant life to be lived by faith in the Lord Jesus Christ. My whole soul was afire with my discovery, and I could scarcely think or talk of anything else. I had found out something about the salvation of Christ of which I had never even dreamed, something that proved Him to be a far more complete Savior than I could have conceived of.

I saw that He was not only my Savior for the future, but He was also my all-sufficient Savior for the present. He was my Captain to fight my battles for me, in order that I need not fight them myself; He was my Burden-bearer to carry my burdens, in order that I might roll them off of my own weak shoulders; He was my Fortress to hide me from my enemies; my Shield to protect me; my Guide to lead me; my Comforter to console me; my Shepherd to care for me. No longer did I need to care for, and protect, and fight for myself. It was all in the hands of One who was mighty to save; and what could I do but trust Him?

No words can express the fullness and the all-sufficiency that I saw was stored up for me in the Lord.

I could not keep such glorious news to myself. Every one who came within the range of my influence was obliged to listen to my story.

One of the first to be told was the cousin whom I have mentioned a little way back, as being surprised at my teaching of the necessity of a continual bondage to sin, in spite of the fact that there was full forgiveness for all our sins, past, present, and to come. I seized the earliest opportunity I could find to have a visit from her, and, on her arrival, greeted her with the words, "Oh, Carrie, I have something so wonderful to tell you. We must not lose a minute before I begin."

As soon as we could get alone I poured out to her my new discovery, telling her I had found out that there was in Christ, not only forgiveness for sin, but also deliverance from its power, and that we need not any longer be the "slaves of sin," but might be more than conquerors through Him.

My cousin listened with amazed interest, her face growing more astonished and perplexed every minute, and when at last I paused to take breath, she burst out—"But Hannah, what *do* you mean? You have always told me that even although you were a child of God you could not expect to be delivered from sin, or from worries, because the old Adam was too strong for you, and the new nature could not conquer the old. Why on earth," she asked with indignant remonstrance, "have you let me go on all this long time with that idea? When I was converted I fully expected to be delivered from sin, and from all worrying and unrest of soul, but when I talked to you about it, you said it was impossible in this life; and I thought of course you knew, and so I gave up all hope of it. And now here you say exactly the opposite. It certainly is very confusing, and I really do not know what to think."

I agreed with her that it was confusing, but that after all it had only been ignorance in the old days that had made possible such a false view of things as I had then taught, and that now I had discovered something far better in the gospel of Christ, and that all we had to do was to throw the old false view overboard, and accept the new truth that had been shown us. My cousin, who had all along had an instinct, in spite of all that was said, that the other way could not be the best the salvation of the Lord Jesus Christ had to offer, embraced with avidity this new teaching of deliverance from temptation through the Lord Jesus Christ, and carried it out far more faithfully than I did.

The practical working of my new discovery amazed me. I committed the whole matter of my rebellious spirit to the Lord, and told Him *I* could not conquer it, but that I believed *He* could conquer it for me; and then I stood aside, as it were, and left the battle to Him. And to my indescribable joy I found all my rebellion taken away, and such a spirit of peaceful acquiescence in the will of God put into its place, that the life which had before looked so utterly distasteful to me, began to look pleasant and even desirable. I found I could say, "Thy will be done" heartily and with thankfulness. My discovery proved itself to be a practical success and I was enchanted.

In numberless ways I tested it and it never failed. One striking instance I remember vividly. I had been imposed upon in what I felt to be a most unjustifiable way, and in what I can see now, in looking back, was really unjustifiable, and I felt very much aggrieved, and was tempted to go into a fit of sulks and to show my displeasure by being sulky for a week or two. But, immediately, when the temptation came, a sight of the way of escape came also, and I rushed off to be alone somewhere that I might fight the battle out. I remember that I was so boiling over with provocation that I could not walk quietly, but fairly ran up to my bedroom, slamming the doors after me. When safe in the seclusion of my room, I kneeled down and said, "Lord, I am provoked, I want to be provoked, and I think I have cause for being provoked; but I know I ought not to be, and I want the victory. I hand this whole matter over to Thee. I cannot fight this battle. Thou must fight it for me. Jesus saves me now." I said these words out of a heart that seemed brimful of rebellion. According to all appearances I was declaring a lie when I said the Lord saved me, for I was not saved, and it did not look likely I could be.

But by faith I laid hold of it, and declared even in the midst of turmoil that the Lord could and did save me now. The result was that immediately a summer morning of peace and happiness spread over me. All my resentment and provocation vanished, and I felt as happy as a bird in the sunshine at the thought of the very thing which before had made me so angry. My faith had laid hold of a divine fact. I had proved that God was able to deliver, and that He did deliver the soul that trusted Him. I realized that it was a wonderful truth that I had no need to fight my own battles, for the Lord fought for me, and I could hold my peace.

Many hundreds of similar battles have been fought and won for me since by the Captain of my Salvation, and the secret I learned then, of handing over the battle to the Lord, and leaving it in His hands, has never failed to work when I have acted on it. It has been to me over and over a practical illustration of Christ's words, "Be of good cheer, for I have overcome the world." *He* has overcome it, not *we* ; and He will always overcome it when we will put the matter into His hands, and will stand aside and let Him fight. Never once, when I have done this, have I been disappointed; for it is blessedly true, although so few seem to know it, that He *is* able to save them to the uttermost that come unto God by Him, seeing He ever liveth to make intercession for them. He was able then, when the Epistle to the Hebrews was written, and He is able now; for He is not dead, but "ever liveth" to make intercession for us.

I had discovered that faith is the conquering law of the universe. God spake, and it was done, and, relying upon Him, we too may speak and it shall be done. A wonderful light streamed upon 1 John

5:14, 15. "And this the confidence that we have in Him, that if we ask anything according to His will, He heareth us: and if we know that He hear us, whatsoever we ask, we know that we have the petitions that we desired of Him." I had always hitherto thought of this passage as one of those beautiful dreams of the Christian life that nobody, in their senses, supposed for a moment was meant to be realized in this world; but now I saw it was no dream, but was simply the statement of a Divine law, the law of faith; a law as certain in its action as the law of gravitation, if only one understood it.

Our Lord tells us over and over that according to our faith it shall be unto us, and actually asserts, without any limitations, that all things are possible to him that believeth; but I had never supposed this was anything more than a romance. Now I saw that He had been simply enunciating a law of the spiritual kingdom, which any one might try and prove for themselves. I saw that faith links us to the Almighty power of God, and makes it possible for our weakness to draw down unfailing supplies of His strength; and there seemed no limit to its possibilities.

> "Faith, mighty faith, the promise sees
>   And looks at that alone;
> Laughs at impossibilities,
>   And cries, It shall be done."

I wish I could say that I have always since lived in the power of this divine law of faith. But one thing I can say, that whenever and wherever I have chosen to lay hold by faith of God's strength, it has always been made perfect in my weakness, and I have had the victory; and over and over I have been able to say with the apostle, "In all these things we are more than conquerors through Him that loved us."

CHAPTER NINETEEN

A DISCOVERY, NOT AN ATTAINMENT

*A*gain I want to make the fact clear that, just as it was before, what had come to me now was a discovery, and in no sense an attainment. I had not become a better woman than I was before, but I had found out that Christ was a better Savior than I had thought He was. I was not one bit more able to conquer my temptations than I had been in the past, but I had discovered that He was able and willing to conquer them for me. I had no more wisdom or righteousness of my own than I had ever had, but I had found out that He could really and actually be made unto me, as the Apostle declared He would be, wisdom, and righteousness, and sanctification, and redemption.

I shall never forget the first time this declaration was proved to me to be, not only a pious saying, but a downright fact. Shortly after I had come to know something of the fullness of Christ's salvation, an occasion arose in my life when I realized that I should have need of a very large amount of patience. An individual, who was especially antagonistic to me, was coming to spend two weeks at our house. She had always in the past been very provoking and irritating, and I felt, as the day drew near for her arrival, that, if I was to behave to her in a really Christ-like way, I should need a far greater supply of patience that I usually possessed. As I was still new in the way of faith, I supposed I could only secure a sufficient supply by wrestling for it in prayer, and I decided, as my days were very busy ones, to devote a whole night before her arrival to the wrestling necessary to secure enough patience to last me throughout the two weeks of her stay. Therefore one night, after the rest of the family had retired, I shut myself up in my room, taking with me a plate of biscuits, which I had provided in case I should be hungry; and, kneeling down by my bed, I prepared myself for an all-night conflict. I confess I felt rather like a martyr, for I had always found long times of prayer very fatiguing; but a stock of patience was a necessity, and I supposed this was the only way to get it. I seemed to picture it to myself something as if a great lump of patience was to be let down into my heart, from which I could break off a bit to use whenever the need should arise. But scarcely had my knees touched the floor when, like a flash, there came into my mind the declaration to which I have referred, "But of Him are ye in Christ Jesus, who of God is made unto us wisdom, and righteousness, and sanctification, and redemption; that, according as it is written, He that glorieth, let Him glory in the Lord." "Yes," I exclaimed inwardly, "and of course patience as well!" And I rose at once from my knees, with an absolute conviction that I did not in the least need, as I had thought, to lay in a big stock of patience to use during my friend's visit, but that I could simply, as the occasion arose, look to the Lord for a present supply for my present need. I seemed to see Christ as a great storehouse of supplies, from which I could draw whatever grace or strength I required; and I realized that it was utter folly for me to try and carry about with me stocks of grace, as it were in packages in my pocket, which, even if I could secure them, would be sure to be mislaid just when I needed them most.

It followed as a matter of course, that my faith was fully answered; and, although my friend was more aggravating than ever, the necessary patience was always supplied at every moment of her stay. And, what was even better than this especial deliverance, I had learned the magnificent fact that the inexhaustible storehouse of God's supplies lies always open to the needs and claims of His children. My patience in this case might be called an attainment by some, but I had not attained it, I had simply discovered a supply of patience in the Divine Storehouse, and by faith I had taken possession hour by hour of what that hour required.

When reduced to its final analysis, the discovery I had made was simply this, that there was stored up for me in Christ a perfect supply for all my needs, and that faith and faith only was the channel through which this supply could flow; that struggling, and wrestling, and worrying, and agonizing, cannot bring this supply, but that faith always will and always does. This seems a very simple discovery to have made, and one would suppose every child of God, who reads the Bible and believes it, would necessarily know it. But I for one did not know it, even after nine years of careful Bible study, and of earnest Christian striving, and when I did at last discover it, it revolutionized my life.

There was no mystery about it. It was not something added on to the gospel story, but was only the real meaning of the Gospel. Christ came, according to the Bible, to accomplish certain purposes; and the discovery I had made was simply that He might be depended on actually to accomplish these purposes. It goes without saying that, if this is the fact, then those who want these purposes accomplished, should hand them over to the One who has undertaken to do it; and to me this seemed then, and has seemed ever since, not any especial religious attainment, but only good sound ordinary common sense.

When I call in a builder to build me a house, I do so because he knows how to build, and is able to accomplish it, while I neither know how nor am able. But I do not consider the fact of my putting the work into his hands as an attainment on my part, but only as a common-sense arrangement. If I am puzzled how to cross a roaring river, and discover a bridge, I do not call my action in crossing that bridge an attainment, but simply and only a most common-sense proceeding.

Consequently it always seems to me much nearer the truth to use the word gifts rather than the word attainments. Attainments imply work and effort on our part, and Christian graces are all a free gift from God. Those who are to "reign in life" are not those who attain to great heights of piety, but those who "receive abundance of grace, and the gift of righteousness." He that spared not His own Son, but delivered Him up for us all, how shall He not with Him also freely give us all things? "Therefore let no man glory in men; for all things are yours; whether Paul or Apollos, or the world, or life, or death, or things present, or things to come; all are yours and ye are Christ's, and Christ is God's." To find out that all things are really ours, is not an attainment but a magnificent discovery, and the soul that makes it would be amazingly lacking in common sense not to take possession of everything it needs.

It would take the pen of an angel to tell all that this discovery meant to me. But suffice it to say that life was transformed, and that where failure and defeat reigned before, victory and triumph became, whenever I chose to lay hold of them by faith, my daily and hourly portion. I was no longer the "slave of sin," compelled whether I would or no to obey it, but had entered into the "liberty wherewith Christ hath made us free," and did not need to be "entangled again with the old yoke of bondage." I thought I was happy before, but my happiness now was such as could not be described in words, and it often seemed to me that even Heaven itself could hardly have more to offer. But my joy was joy in the Lord, and not joy in myself, nor in any attainments of my own, for I had none. I understood what the prophet meant when he said, "Thus saith the Lord, let not the wise man glory in his wisdom, neither let the mighty man glory in his might; let not the rich man glory in his riches: but let him that glorieth glory in this that he understandeth and knoweth Me, that I am the Lord which exercise loving kindness, judgment, and righteousness, in the earth; for in these things I delight, saith the Lord."

I had no wisdom, nor might, nor riches to glory in, but I was learning to know the Lord, and in Him I could glory with all my heart.

"Where is boasting then?" asks the Apostle. And he answers in words that now at last I understood, "It is excluded. By what law? of works? Nay but by the law of faith." How can the soul boast of its attainments, when it has none; and how can it fail to make its boast in the Lord when He so freely bestows upon it the supply for all its needs? "For by grace are ye saved through faith; and that not of yourselves; it is the gift of God: not of works, lest any man should boast." "For they got not the land in possession by their own sword, neither did their own arm save them; but thy right hand, and thine arm, and the light of thy countenance, because thou hadst a favor unto them."

This was my experience, and with all my heart I could unite in the words of the Psalmist—"In God we boast all the day long, and praise Thy Name forever!"

CHAPTER TWENTY

THE SECRET OF A HAPPY LIFE

*T*his new life I had entered upon has been called by several different names. The Methodists called it "The Second Blessing," or "The Blessing of Sanctification"; the Presbyterians called it "The Higher Life," or "The Life of Faith"; the Friends called it "The Life hid with Christ in God." But by whatever name it may be called, the truth at the bottom of each name is the same, and can be expressed in four little words, "Not I, but Christ." In every case it means that we abandon ourselves to the Lord for Him to work in us, both to will and to do of His good pleasure, that we take Him to be our Savior from the power of sin as well as from its punishment, and that we trust Him to give us, according to His promise, grace to help in every time of need.

Personally I prefer to call it "The life of faith," as being more simple. But, in that book of mine, in which I have most fully set it forth, I have called it the "Secret of a Happy Life,"[1] for the reason that it was for so long a secret from myself, and because it is, I fear,

[1]Fleming H. Revell Company, 158 Fifth Avenue, New York; James Nisbet & Co., L't'd, 21 Berners St., London.

still a secret from hundreds of God's children, who are groaning under the same grievous burdens as I once had to carry. It was not a secret in the sense that God had hidden it, but only a secret in the sense that I had not discovered it. It was and is an open secret, spread wide out before all eyes in the Bible, if only I had had the spiritual discernment to see it.

> "The secrets of the gods are from of old,
>   Guarded forever, and forever told;—
>   Blabbed in all ears, but published in a tongue
>   Whose purport the gods only can unfold."

An ox and a philosopher may look at the same field, but they will not see the same things there; and my eyes, before and after this glorious discovery, looked at the same Bible, and even read the same passages, but saw very different things. The Bible like nature lies open to all, but not all see it. The law of gravitation was working plainly before all men, but only Newton saw it. And similarly the law of faith was plainly shown in the Bible, although my eyes had failed to discern it. The forces we use in nature were not created by us, but only discovered. They existed as much before they were discovered as afterwards. And no discoverers of Nature's secrets have ever, I am sure, had greater delight in their discoveries, than I have had in my discovery of the "Secrets of God."

So great was my delight that I felt impelled to speak of it to everybody, and to compel every one to listen.

At first my husband, who was an earnest and successful Christian worker, felt somewhat frightened lest I might be rejoicing in some heresy that would do myself and others harm; and he continually fell back on the argument that the "old man" in us could never be entirely conquered in this life, but must always bring us more or less into bondage. One morning, when we were arguing the matter, I said, "Well, impossible or not, it is certainly in the Bible; and I would like to know what thee thinks of this passage in the sixth of Romans—'Knowing this, that our old man is crucified with Him, that the body of sin might be destroyed, that henceforth we should not serve sin.' What can this mean?" I said, "but that the body, that is, the power of sin, is really to be conquered, so that we no longer need to serve sin?" Startled by the new light that seemed suddenly to shine out of these words, he exclaimed: "There is no such passage in the Bible." "Oh, yes, there is," I replied; and, turning to my Bible, I showed it to him. It was a passage with which, of course, he had been very familiar, but which now appeared to him with such an absolutely new meaning that he felt as if he had never seen it before. It brought conviction, however; and from that time he did not rest until he had discovered the truth for himself.

His own account of this discovery, published in 1868, was as follows. After telling of the lack he had been feeling in his Christian life, he says:—

"I knew, however, that the Bible seemed to contemplate a better life for the Christian than this, and for some years the impression had been increasing upon my mind that there was some part of the truth of God that I had missed of finding. . . . I felt that in the truth, as I held it, there was a painful want of that spirit of love which is the uniting bond of the Church of Christ, and which the Scriptures declare is so much more and better than "all knowledge" and "all faith"; and I often expressed my growing conviction that there was some truth yet to break out of God's Word that would fill our hearts with a love that could bear all things. So strong was this feeling that I had arranged for a meeting of some brethren, well versed in the Scriptures, to carefully examine together and in detail what part of God's Word we had failed to receive and to teach. Circumstances delayed this meeting, but in the meantime, through an unlooked-for channel, I was to receive the secret, that was to teach me the joy of Christian liberty, and the power of true service. That secret was faith! Strange! that when I had so constantly taught faith as the appointed channel for the forgiveness of sins, I had failed to see that faith alone was also the means of deliverance from the inward power of sin. Not the sinner only, but the Christian also, must receive everything by faith.

"I met at this time some Christians whose inward life, as they described it, seemed to be very different from mine. They declared that practical sanctification was to be obtained, like justification, by simple faith; and that, like justification, it was to be realized in any moment in which our faith should be able to grasp it; and they declared further that they themselves had experienced it. The subject was continually brought to my attention, and over and over again proofs were brought from the Word, to which I professed to be, and verily thought I was, in such entire subjection. But I regarded the whole thing with a deep feeling of distress, for it seemed to me that what they were aiming after and professing to have attained was a perfection of the flesh, and *that* I knew was impossible. I scarcely know anything towards which I had such a deep-rooted prejudice, and I suffered many hours of anxiety in thinking over the sad consequences of this heresy which I saw creeping in among us. So determined was my opposition; that even familiar passages of Scripture, when quoted to prove that sanctification was by faith, and that it was possible to walk worthy of the Lord unto all pleasing, assumed such unfamiliar aspects that I could scarcely believe they were in the Bible at all.

"One morning, Rom. 6:6, was quoted to me with the remark that when God said of the believer that his 'old man is crucified with Christ that the body of sin might be destroyed, that henceforth we should not serve sin,' it certainly must mean something, and something too which would make it possible for a believer no longer to be the slave of sin. I was so astonished at the force of the words that I said at once and emphatically, 'That passage is not in the Bible,' although as a fact there were but few that were more familiar. And then, when forced to acknowledge that it was there, I took refuge in the plea that it was only judicial—that is, true in God's sight, but never actually true in the Christian's experience. But from that moment I began to wonder whether there might not be after all some truth in what they were teaching; and slowly I discovered that I had misapprehended their meaning. It was not a perfection in the flesh that they were talking of, but a death of the flesh, and a life hid in Christ,—a life of abiding and walking in Him, and therefore a life of victory and triumph, and one well pleasing to God.

"'But is that *all* you mean?' I asked at one time, when this had been especially pressed upon me. 'That is nothing new. I have always known it.'

"'But have you *lived* it?' was the question asked.

"'Yes,' I replied, 'I have often lived so. Very often I have given myself up entirely into the care of the Lord, and have realized that I was dead, and that He alone lived in me.'

"'You have realized this as an occasional experience,' was the answer to this, 'but have you realized it as a *life*? You say you have taken refuge in the Lord sometimes, but have you ever taken up your abode in Him?'

"I saw that I had not. My faith had been very intermittent in this respect. In circumstances of peculiar difficulty, or where I had from any cause felt especially weak in myself, I had had resource to the Lord exclusively, and had always found Him at such times sufficient for my utmost need. But that this occasional experience might be and ought to be the experience of my whole life, I had never dreamed.

"'What would you think,' asked my friend, 'of people who should trust Christ in this intermittent way for the salvation of their souls'—who should one week realize their own power-lessness to do anything towards it, and should therefore trust it altogether and wholly to the Lord, but should the next week try to do it partly themselves, asking His help to make up what was lacking in their own efforts? Would not such a course seem to you utterly foolish and inconsistent? And yet is it not equally inconsistent, and equally dishonoring to the Lord, for you to trust Him for your daily living in this inter-mittent way, sometimes walking by faith, and sometimes by your own efforts?'

"I could not but acknowledge the truth of this, and the pos-sibilities and blessedness of a life of continual faith began to dawn upon me."

Such was my husband's account of his discovery; and to my great joy we were both from this time forward of one accord in regard to it.

It was not that either he or I considered ourselves to have be-come sinless, or that we never met with any further failures. We had simply discovered the "secret of victory," and knew that we were no longer the "slaves of sin" and therefore forced to yield to its mastery, but that we might, if we would, be made more than conquerors through our Lord Jesus Christ. But this did not mean that temptations ceased to come; and when we neglected to avail ourselves of the "secret" we had discovered, and, instead of hand-ing the battle over to the Lord, took it into our own hands as of old, failure inevitably followed.

But we had learned that it was really a fact that the Lord was both able and willing to deliver us out of every temptation, if we would but trust Him to do it; and we saw that our old idea that we were necessarily the "servants of sin" was contrary to the Scriptures, and was a libel on the completeness of the salvation of Christ, who had died on purpose to deliver us from its bondage. "For sin shall not have dominion over you: for you are not under the law, but under grace." And we had discovered further that faith, and faith only, was the road to victory, and that effort and wrestling were of no avail in this battle. Our part, we saw, was simply surrender and faith, and God's part was to do all the rest.

For a third time, as I have said, a skin was peeled off the Bible, and on every page we found the "secret of victory" set forth in letters of light. As before, the old texts took on a deeper and a fuller meaning. Take for instance the passage, "For whatsoever is born of God overcometh the world, and this is the victory that overcometh the world, even our faith. Who is he that overcometh the world but he that believeth that Jesus is the Son of God." This had been one of our favorite passages, but we had taken it to mean only a future overcoming, when death should be swallowed up in victory, and we should overcome the world by leaving it behind us. Now we saw that it meant a present overcoming of the world, by the power of a present faith, while still living in it.

Or take this passage, "Behold the Lamb of God that taketh away the sin of the world." This had meant to us heretofore the taking away of the future penalty of sin, but now we saw that it meant taking away its present power, so that we need no longer serve it or be a bond slave to it.

I might multiply innumerable instances of this unveiling of the Bible under our new light, but these will suffice. We had made a transforming discovery, and it filled our every thought.

It seemed to me such an amazing and delightful thing that, as I have said, I could not keep it to myself. Whenever I met any of my friends my first question would be, "How much time have you to spare, for I have something splendid to tell you." And I would at once proceed to pour out my tale of the great salvation I had discovered. To most of my friends it was as new and delightful as it had been to me, and many of them took hold of it at once as an experimental reality. But one of them, the friend who had been the means of my awakening at sixteen, and who had been my closest religious confidante ever since, after listening to my story, said, "But, Hannah, that is nothing new. I have always known it." "Then why," I asked in great indignation, "did you never tell me about it? Here have I been, as you must have known, struggling along all these years with my temptations, having a few victories perhaps, but a far greater number of defeats, and all the while you knew of a secret of victory and yet never told me. How could you be so unkind?" "But of course I thought you knew it," she replied. "It is what the Quakers have always taught. Their preaching is almost altogether about it. I thought every Christian knew it." "Well," I said, "every Christian does not know it, and very few, in fact, do know it. Most Christians believe that they are obliged, owing to the weakness of the flesh, to be the 'servants of sin' all their lives; and most of them think that in order to get any victory at all, they have got to fight and wrestle for it themselves; and they never see that the Bible declares that victory is given to faith and to faith only. I feel sure," I added, "that nearly all Christians believe, as I did, that they must do all the fighting themselves, but that, if defeat seems imminent, they can then ask the Lord to come to their help. But they do not in the least understand that what they are to do is to hand the battle over to Him in the very beginning, while they 'stand still and see the salvation of the Lord,' just as the children of Israel did at the Red Sea. Moses told the Israelites then that the Lord would fight for them, and they might hold their peace, and I think everybody who knows about it ought to tell people the same thing now. And," I added emphatically, as I bade my friend good-bye, "I for one mean to tell it wherever I can."

Consequently no one, whether old or young, whether an advanced Christian or a young beginner, to whom I dared speak, failed to hear the story, and, one after another, nearly all my friends accepted it and began to live in the power of it.

Among the rest was my own little daughter, who was at this time about seven or eight years old. She had begun to develop a spirit of great willfulness which I had found very hard to control. She herself recognized that it was wrong, and tried to conquer it, but she seemed somehow possessed. One day she came to me with a very puzzled air and said, "Mother, what *is* the reason I am so naughty? I know I am a little Christian girl, and I thought Christians were always good; but though I try as hard as I can to make myself good, I just can't help being naughty." I could sympathize with the child from my own experience, and I said, "I expect, darling, that the reason is just because you do try to make yourself good. We never can make ourselves good, let us try as hard as we may. Only our Heavenly Father can make us good, and we must just trust Him to do it. Whenever you feel tempted to be naughty, if you will tell

Him all about it, and ask Him to make you good, and then will trust Him to do it, He will be sure to take all your naughty away." The child remained silent for a while, and then said thoughtfully, "Oh I did not know *that*. I always thought you had to put your will into it, and just do it yourself." And she walked thoughtfully away, having evidently got hold of an entirely new idea.

I very soon noticed a great change in her; all her willfulness seemed to have disappeared, and she was as biddable and gentle as a lamb. I said nothing, as I did not want to intrude roughly into delicate ground, but two or three days afterwards, as she was sitting on the floor of her nursery playing with her dolls, I heard her saying softly to herself, in a tone of subdued exultation, "Oh, I am so glad Heavenly Father is making me so good. It feels so nice to be good." Still I said nothing, but a few nights later, when I was tucking her up in bed she burst out with, "Oh, mother, aren't you glad Heavenly Father is making me so good? He is going to make me a great deal gooder, but aren't you glad He has made me as good as He has this far?" Then, as I hugged and kissed her, and rejoiced with her, she added solemnly, "Mother, do you tell everybody about this?" I replied that I tried to, but she was not satisfied, and said, "But, mother, you must not only try to, you must really do it every time you preach, for I expect there are lots of people like I was, who want to be good and don't know how, and you ought to tell every single person you meet." I have always taken this as a sort of Divine call for my work.

In fact, however, our hearts were so full of the subject that we needed no incentive to fulfill our little daughter's injunction, and everybody we knew did sooner or later hear our story. As a consequence a great stir was created in our own circle, and I may say all over the Church in America as well, and even in England. Inquiries began to come from all quarters as to what this new doctrine, taught by the Pearsall Smiths at Millville, New Jersey, could be; and very soon meetings and conferences began to be held in various places, many of which, are still held to this day, and are generally called "Meetings for the deepening of the spiritual life." I shall hope to give a full account of this movement elsewhere.

Suffice it to say here that this discovery, which I have tried to set forth, was the beginning of a great revival in the spiritual life of the Church everywhere. It reached its culmination in the meetings held in 1873 and 1874 on the Continent, and at Oxford and Brighton, when thousands of Christians came from all quarters to hear the story; and the effects of which are still felt in numberless lives. I never go anywhere that I do not meet people who tell me that their whole lives were changed by what they learned at those meetings. It was not that they had found a new religion, but only that their old religion had become vital to them, and the things they had before thought they believed, had been made actual and living realities. They had *called* Christ their Savior, but now they had learned to know that He really did save, and they had trusted Him to do it, and He had not failed them.

There had been nothing Sectarian in the teaching, and there had been no need for any one to change their Creed or their denomination. In all denominations, even where in other respects they may seem to hold widely diverging views, there have always been those who have understood and lived the life of faith, not only among the Methodists, but among the Quakers and among the Catholics as well, and in fact it is I believe at the bottom of the creeds of every Church. All that is needed therefore is for the members of each Church to give up merely *professing* their beliefs, and begin actually to *believe* them; and, in believing them, they will always find them to be true.

It is a blessed fact about the life of faith that, no matter what the Creed or what the denomination, it fits into all, and the story is everywhere the same.

CHAPTER TWENTY ONE

HOLINESS CAMP MEETINGS

*A*s may be imagined, we took every possible opportunity of learning all we could of the new truths we had discovered; and I must confess that, although we found, as I have said, that the Friends did actually teach it, yet it was among the Methodists we received the clearest light. The Methodists were very definite about it. They taught definitely that there were two experiences in the Christian life, the first being justification, and the second sanctification, and they urged Christians not to be satisfied with justification (*i.e.*, forgiveness) merely, but also to seek sanctification or the "second blessing," as they called it, as well. I should not myself express the truth in this fashion now, but at that time I must acknowledge it was most helpful.

It was not, however, every Methodist who took this ground, as many thought it was too extreme. Those who did were called "Holiness Methodists," and it was from them we received the most help. They held "Holiness Meetings" for the express purpose of considering the subject and it was our delight to attend these Meetings whenever we could. Especially did we enjoy their "Holiness Camp Meetings," which were held in the summer time in lonely forests or at seaside places. They were called "Meetings for the promotion of holiness," and were really great open air Conferences of Christians of all denominations, from all parts of the country, who were interested in the subject, and who would assemble at these Camp Meetings, living in tents under the trees, and spending a week or ten days in waiting upon God, and conferring together on the deep things of the Kingdom.

No words can express the wonderful power, and solemnity, and yet overwhelming joyfulness, of these meetings. We were there living in tents, entirely separated from all our usual occupations and cares, with nothing to do but to give ourselves up to the spiritual influences around us, and to open our hearts to what we believed to be the teachings of the Holy Spirit. Such a company of earnest Christians, all set on coming into a closer communion with God, could not fail to create a spiritual atmosphere of great intensity; and the thrilling experiences of spiritual joy that were told in every meeting, with the songs of praise resounding through the forest, and the happy faces of every one we met, were all something so out of the ordinary and so entrancing, that it often seemed almost as if we were on the very threshold of Heaven. I cannot help pitying every Christian who has known nothing of such seasons of pure delight. They were a sort of culmination of the grand spiritual romance which my religion has always been to me, and I count them among the most entrancing times of my life. To this day the sight of a camp chair, or of a tent under the trees, always brings back to me something of the old sense of supreme happiness that used to fill every hour of those delicious Camp Meetings.

A friend of ours who knew nothing of the especial object of the Meetings, having heard that we were attending one of them, came unexpectedly to see what it was like. He arrived early in the morning, and on the way to our tent met the people returning from the early Prayer Meeting. He was profoundly impressed with their looks of peace and joy, and he said to us, "What is the matter with all these people, that their faces shine so? Nearly everybody I have seen on this Camp ground seems to have a shining face; but I met a few whose faces did not shine, and I want to know what is the difference." We told him as well as we could, that the "shining faces" were an index of hearts at rest in the Lord, while those whose faces did not shine had not yet learned the blessed secret. He listened to us with the deepest interest, and, when we had done, he said with conviction, "Well I am determined that I too will get a 'shining face,' and I will stay on this Camp ground until I do." And sure enough, in a few days his face too was shining with the joys of God's salvation.

I shall never forget the first time I was present at one of these Camp Meetings, and the first Prayer Meeting I attended. It was an early morning meeting in a tent. I knew nothing of Methodist Meetings, having never attended any except those little ones at Millville, and had no conception of the emotional atmosphere into which I had come. I found when I got into the meeting that I had forgotten my handkerchief, but having never in my life shed any tears in a meeting, I was not troubled. But in this meeting the fountains of my being seemed to be broken up, and floods of delicious tears poured from my eyes. I was reduced to great straits, and was obliged surreptitiously to lift up my dress and use my white under-skirt to dry my tears. I have never since been to any meeting without at least two handkerchiefs safely tucked away in my pocket, although I believe I have never since been so overwhelmed with emotion as at that time. It was my first introduction to the entrancing joys of spiritual emotion, and I reveled in it.

As I left the tent where the meeting had been held, a Methodist "Holiness Sister," seeing my emotion, put her arm around me, and told me of her own experience in sanctification, and took me in hand to help me. Guided by her, I soon found myself in the way of getting the full benefit of all the exercises of the meetings. I found that they talked a great deal about what they called the "blessing of sanctification," and at every meeting we were urged to come forward to what they called the "altar" (which was really a bench set apart for the purpose) to seek for this "blessing." Just what the "blessing" was I did not understand, but it seemed to be something very tangible, which resulted from entire consecration and simple faith, and which made people rapturously happy. My "Holiness Sister" soon had me going forward to the "altar" to obtain this "blessing." I was determined to get whatever there was to be had, and I was more and more fired with enthusiasm by the thrilling testimonies I continually heard on every hand from those who had received the "blessing," so that I was nothing loth to embrace every opportunity for going to the "altar" to seek it. In fact I enjoyed doing so immensely, for it seemed somehow to bring me to the delicious verge of unknown spiritual possibilities, that might at any moment reveal themselves.

Apart, however, from this treading as it were, on the threshold, no especial "blessing" ever came to me from these visits to the "altar." I am not of an emotional nature, and none of the overpowering emotions I heard described, as constituting the "blessing," ever fell to my portion. But the grand truth that was taught at these Meetings, that the Lord Jesus Christ was a Savior from the power of sin as well as a Savior from the guilt of sin, became more and more real and effective to me; but of any blessing, as a blessing, apart from the truth, I realized nothing. A knowledge of the truth was all the blessing I ever received; and although at first I was somewhat disappointed, I came in time to see that a knowledge of the truth was all the "blessing" I needed. And I was gradually convinced that a large part of what was called "the blessing" was simply the emotional response of emotional natures to the discovery of a magnificent truth. To me it came with intellectual conviction and delight, to more emotional natures it came with emotional conviction and delight, but in both cases the truth was the same, and it was the truth, not the emotion, that set the soul free.

I have many times since noticed this difference in people's experiences; and I have also noticed that, very often the emotional experiences have not been as solid and permanent as the more intellectual ones. In the very nature of things emotions are more or less variable, while convictions, where they are really convictions, and are not purely notions or ideas, are permanent. Once convince a man that two and two make four, and no amount of dyspepsia or east wind can change his conviction; while everything that is only a matter of feeling, and not of conviction, is at the mercy of these and a thousand other untoward influences. I learned in time therefore not to seek emotions, but to seek only for convictions, and I found to my surprise and delight that my convictions brought me a far more stable and permanent joy than many of my more emotional friends seemed to experience. In the time of stress, with many of them, their emotions flagged, and even often vanished, and they had hard fights to prevent utter failure and despair, and some of them have been thankful at last to struggle back to the stable ground of conviction, which in their emotional days had seemed so barren and comfortless.

All this however took me many years in learning. But meanwhile the joy and power of the glorious secret we had discovered grew every year more and more practical; and more and more my soul learned to rest in absolute confidence on the keeping and saving power of the Lord. I must repeat what I have said elsewhere, that not for a moment do I mean that temptation ceased its attacks, or that we had reached what is sometimes called "sinless perfection." Temptations continued to arise, and sometimes failures befell. But we had discovered a "way to escape," and had learned that this way was the way of faith. We had found out that Christ was a Deliverer, not only from the future punishment for sin, but from the present power of sin, and we realized that we need no longer be the "slaves of sin." And just so far as we laid hold by faith of this deliverance, just so far were we delivered. We had not picked up holiness and put it into our pockets as a permanent and inalienable possession; but we had discovered the "highway" of holiness, and had learned the secret of walking therein. When we walked there, we had victory, when we tried other pathways, we found failure. It was simply this, that at last, after many years of "wilderness wandering," we had entered into the "promised land" and had found it true as was said to Israel of old that "every place the sole of your foot shall tread upon that have I given you." The whole land was ours, and it only needed for us to "go up and possess it."

We had discovered that the Bible stated a fact when it said, "And God is able to make all grace abound towards you; that ye, always having all sufficiency in all things, may abound to every good work." And we had proved in actual experience that God really *was* able, if only we were willing.

Christ had been revealed to us, not as our future Savior only, but as our present and complete Savior now and here, able to keep us from falling, and to deliver us out of the hands of all our enemies.

For myself I had now entered upon a region of romance before which the glory of all other romances paled into insignificance. It was like an exploration of the very courts of heaven itself. Every day was a fresh revelation. Words fail when I try to describe it. I often in my heart called it the "bird life," for I felt like a bird spreading its wings in a country all sunshine and greenness, and soaring upwards into the blue of an unfathomable sky. In the past, I had been a caged bird, happy in its cage because it knew nothing of the uncaged life outside. But now all barriers seemed removed, and my soul was set free to comprehend with all saints what is the "breadth, and length, and depth, and height; and to know the love of Christ which passeth knowledge."

I thought, when I discovered the restitution of all things, that I had reached this comprehension, but I saw now wider breadths, and longer lengths, and deeper depths, and higher heights, than I had even conceived of then, and the love of Christ that seemed then to pass knowledge, became now an unfathomable abyss of delight.

I had found that God, just God alone, without anything else, was enough. Even the comfort of His promises paled before the comfort of Himself. What difference did it make if I could not find a promise to fit my case? I had found the Promiser, and He was infinitely more than all His promises.

I remember well how, when I was a child and found myself in any trouble or perplexity, the coming in of my father or my mother upon the scene would always bring me immediate relief. The moment I heard the voice of one of them calling my name, that very moment every burden dropped off and every fear vanished. I had got my father or my mother, and what more could I need. It was their simple presence that did it. They did not need to stand up and make a string of promises for my relief, nor detail to me the plans of deliverance. The mere fact of their presence was all the assurance I required that everything now would be all right for me,— must in fact be all right, because they were my parents, and I was their child. And how much more true must all this be in regard to our Heavenly Father, who has all wisdom and all power, and whose very name is the God of Love. His presence is literally and truly all we need for everything. It would be enough for us, even if we had not a single promise nor a single revelation of His plans. How often in the Bible He has settled all the questions and fears of His people by the simple announcement, "I will be with thee." Who can doubt that in that announcement He meant to say that all His wisdom, and all His love, and all His omnipotent power, would therefore of course be engaged on their side?

I was married very young, and knew but little of housekeeping, and would naturally often find myself in bothers and snarls over my household duties, and not know what to do. And then sometimes, in the midst, I would hear the front door bell ring, and my mother's voice would ask, "Is Hannah at home?" And I would exclaim, with a sigh of infinite relief, "Oh, there is mother," and all my troubles would vanish as though they had never been. My mother was there, and would manage it all. And over and over again in my spiritual life the words, "Oh, there is God," have brought me a similar but far more blessed deliverance. With God present what can there be to fear? Since He has said, "I will never leave thee nor forsake thee," every heart that knows Him cannot but boldly say, "I will not fear what man can do unto me."

Every fear, every perplexity, every anxiety, find an all-satisfying answer in God—He Himself, what He is in nature and character. His ways, or His plans, or even His promises, we may misinterpret or misunderstand, but goodness of character we cannot mistake, and it is the character of God that is our resting-place. He can only act according to His character, and therefore what is His character is the one vital thing we need to know. If He is good, and unselfish, and loving, and wise, and just, and, with all this, omnipotent and omnipresent as well, then all must be ordered right for us. It cannot be otherwise. The seen thing may seem to be all wrong, but we know that the seen thing is very often not at all the true thing. What we are able to see is generally only a partial view, and no partial view can be depended on. I may look at a partial view of a winding river, and declare it to be a lake, because no outlet can be *seen*. To witness the outward seeming of a parent's dealing with a child during the hour of lessons, or during the administration of medicine, or during the necessary discipline and training of a child's life, and to see no further than the outside, would give a very untrue idea of a parent's love. One must have, what George MacDonald calls "eyes that can see below surfaces," if one is to do justice either to a good parent or to a good God. But when His utter unselfishness has been discovered, this interior eye is opened, and all difficulties as to the apparent mysteries of His dealings are answered forever.

I can understand the joy with which the Psalmist reiterated over and over the goodness of the God of Israel. "Oh, give thanks unto the Lord, for He is good"; "Oh, trust in the Lord, for He is good"; "Oh that men would praise the Lord for His goodness"; "The earth is full of the goodness of the Lord"; "Come, taste and see that the Lord is good." Living all around Israel were nations whose gods were not good—cruel gods, unjust gods, and, above all, selfish gods, who cared only for themselves and for their own glory, and who were sublimely indifferent to the welfare of their worshipers; and for the Israelites not to be afraid to contrast with these bad gods their own unselfish, and just God, and to be able to declare, without fear of contradiction, that He was a good God, must have given them triumphant delight. And I feel that it is no less of a triumph now, in the midst of a world that misunderstands and maligns Him, to be able, with absolute conviction and assurance to challenge every human being the world over to "Come, taste and see that the Lord is good!"

CHAPTER TWENTY TWO

THE LOVELY
WILL OF GOD

With my eyes thus opened to see the absolute goodness and unselfishness of God, I experienced a complete change of mind in regard to His will. In the past I had looked upon God's will as being against me, now I had found out that it was for me. I had thought it was something to be afraid of, now I saw it was something to be embraced with joy. Formerly it had seemed to me that His will was the terrible instrument of His severity, and that I must do all I could to avert its terrors from swooping down upon my devoted head. Now I saw that it was the instrument of His love, and could only bring upon me all that was kindest and best. I realized that of course it was impossible for the will of unselfish love to be anything but good and kind; and that, since He has all knowledge and all wisdom as well, it must, in the very nature of things, be the best thing the universe could contain; and that no greater bliss could come to any of us, than to have that lovely unselfish will perfectly done in us and for us.

To hide oneself in God's will seemed to me sometimes like hiding in an impregnable fortress of love and care, where no harm could reach me; and sometimes it seemed like a bed of softest down, upon which I could lie down in a delicious and undisturbed rest. I never can put into words all that I began to see of the loveliness, the tenderness, the unselfishness, the infinite goodness of the will of God! I fairly reveled in its sweetness.

It was not that life was to have no more trials, for this wise and loving will might see that trials were a necessary gift of love. Neither was it essential that we should be able to *see* the Divine hand in every trial, since my common sense told me that He must still be there, for a God who is omnipresent could not help being present somewhere, even in a trial, and, being in it, He would of course be there to help and bless.

We are not wise enough to judge as to things, whether they are really in their essence joys or sorrows, but the Lord knows; and, because He loves us with an unselfish and limitless love, He cannot fail to make the apparently hard, or cruel, or even wicked thing, work together for our best good. I say "cannot fail" simply because it is an unthinkable thing to suppose that such a God as ours could do otherwise.

It is no matter who starts our trial, whether man, or devil, or even our own foolish selves, if God permits it to reach us, He has by this permission made the trial His own, and will turn it for us into a chariot of love which will carry our souls to a place of blessing that we could not have reached in any other way. I saw that to the Christian who hides in the fortress of God's will, there can be no "second causes," for nothing can penetrate into that fortress unless the Divine Keeper of the fortress shall give it permission; and this permission, when given, means that He adopts it as being for our best good. Joseph was sold into Egypt by the wickedness of his brethren, but God made their wickedness the chariot that carried Joseph to his place of triumph over the Egyptians.

We may be certain therefore, more certain than we are that the sun will rise to-morrow, that God's will is the most lovely thing the universe contains for us; and this, not because it always looks or seems the best, but because it cannot help being the best, since it is the will of infinite unselfishness and of infinite love.

I began to sing in my heart continually Faber's lovely hymn:

> "I worship Thee, sweet Will of God,
> And all Thy ways adore;
> And every day I live it seems
> I love Thee more and more."

One verse in this hymn especially delighted me, because I so often found it practically true.

"I know not what it is to doubt,
   My heart is always gay;
  I run no risks, for, come what will,
   Thou always hast Thy way."

The first time I realized it was as follows. It was three days after the birth of a darling little girl baby, for whom I had longed unspeakably, and who seemed to me the most ineffable treasure ever committed to mortal care. My nurse had been suddenly taken ill, and was obliged to leave, and we had been forced to get in a strange nurse whom I did not know, and whose looks I did not like. It was in the days when trained nurses were far less common than now, and I felt sure this one was unusually ignorant. I could hardly endure to have her touch my precious treasure, and yet I was not allowed to care for my darling myself.

It was winter time, and there was a blazing wood fire on the hearth in my sick room. On the first evening of her arrival, the nurse, after settling me in for the night, sat down close to the fire taking my darling baby on her knees. Pretty soon she fell sound asleep, and I was awakened by her snores to see my darling lying perilously near the fire on her slanting lap, while her head nodded over it in what seemed to me like a drunken slumber. I tried in vain to awaken her, but my voice was feeble, and made no impression, and I expected every minute to see my darling baby roll off her lap into the fire. I could make no one hear, and I knew to get out of bed and go across the cold floor might seriously injure me. But my anxiety was so overpowering that I sat up in bed and was just trying to rise, when these words flashed into my mind—"I run no risks, for come what will Thou always hast Thy way." And with it came a conviction that my baby could not run any risks for she was safe in God's care. With a sense of infinite peace my head fell back on my pillow, and my soul sank back on the sweet and lovely will of God. I saw that my darling was cradled in the arms of Almighty love, and I went to sleep without a care, and waked up to find her being comfortably tucked in beside me for her needed meal.

It was lovely beyond words to have had such a practical insight into the beauty and the blessedness of the Will of God!

I have had many such insights since, and I have learned to know beyond the shadow of doubt, that the will of God is the most delicious and delightful thing in the universe. And this, not because things always go as I want them to go, neither because of any extra piety on my part, but simply because my common sense tells me that the will of unselfish love could not be anything else but delightful. The reason heaven is heaven is because God's will is perfectly done there, and earth would necessarily be like heaven, if only His will could be perfectly done here.

I had been used to hear Christians talk about consecration to the will of God as being such a high religious attainment that only a few extra devout souls could hope to reach it. But with my discovery of the infinite unselfishness of God, I came to realize that consecration to Him was not an attainment but a priceless privilege; and I cannot but feel sure that if people only knew the loveliness of His will, not a devout few only, but every single soul in the universe would rush eagerly to choose it for every moment of their lives.

This seems to me to be not an extra degree of piety, but only an extra degree of good common sense. If I were lost in a trackless wilderness and could see no way out, and a skillful guide should offer to lead me into safety, would I consider it a hard thing to surrender myself into his hands, and say, "Thy will be done" to his guidance? And can it be a hard thing to surrender myself to my Heavenly Guide, and say, "Thy will be done" to His guidance? No, a thousand times no! Consecration, or as I prefer to call it, surrender to God, is the greatest privilege offered to any soul in this life, and to say, "Thy will be done" is one of the most delightful things human lips are allowed to utter.

An old writer has said that God's will is not a load to carry, as so many think, but is a pillow to rest on, and I found this to be true. My soul sank back upon it with a sweetness of contented rest that no words can describe. At other times, to say the words "Thy will be done" seemed to me like a magnificent shout of victory, a sort of triumphant banner, flung forth in the face of the whole universe, challenging it to combat. So vividly did I realize this, that it drew from me the only verse of poetry I was ever able to write, which, however poor as poetry, was the heartfelt expression of a very real and inspiring fact.

> "Thy wonderful, grand Will, my God,
> With triumph now I make it mine,

And Love shall cry a joyous *Yes,*
To every dear command of thine."

But time would fail me to tell of all that my soul discovered when I discovered the goodness and unselfishness of God. To say that *He is enough* is to give an absolute and incontrovertible answer to every doubt and every question that has arisen or can arise. It may not seem to our consciousness that any prayers are answered, or any promises fulfilled, but what of that? Behind every prayer and behind every promise, there is God,—the bare God, if I may so express it; and, if He exists at all, we know He must be enough.

How often I had repeated the lines:

"Thou, oh Christ, art all I want,
More than all in Thee I find."

But never until now had I known what they meant. They had seemed to express a beautiful sentiment, but now I saw that they simply stated a fact. I had begun to discover that He actually was all I needed; and that, even infinitely more than all, beyond what I could ask or think, was stored up for me in Him.

In a sense, my search after God was ended, for I had discovered that He was enough!

I have had many blessed and lovely things to find out about Him since, but I had then reached Himself,—the real God, behind all the seemings, and my heart had entered into its rest. I had discovered that nothing else really matters,—neither creeds, nor ceremonies, nor doctrines, nor dogmas. GOD IS; GOD IS UNSELFISH; AND GOD IS ENOUGH!

CHAPTER TWENTY THREE

OLD AGE AND DEATH

*A*nd now that I am seventy years old, and life is rapidly passing from me, if I should be asked how my discovery of the
unselfishness of God affects my feelings towards old age and death,
I can only say, that, secure in the knowledge that God is, and that
He is enough, I find old age delightful in the present, and death a
delicious prospect for the future.

If it were not for Him, old age with its failing powers and its
many infirmities could not but be a sad and wearisome time; but,
with God, our lovely unselfish God, at the back of it, old age is
simply a delightful resting-place. To be seventy gives one permission to stand aloof from the stress of life, and to lay down all burden of responsibility for carrying on the work of the world; and I
rejoice in my immunity.

I have tried in my day to help bear the burdens of my own generation, and, now that that generation has almost passed away, I am
more than happy to know that the responsibilities of the present
generation do not rest upon me, but upon the shoulders of the younger and stronger spirits, who are called in the providence of God to
bear them. I laugh to myself with pleasure at the thought, and quite

enjoy the infirmities of age as they come upon me, and find it delightful to be laid aside from one thing after another, and to be at liberty to look on in a peaceful leisure at the younger wrestlers in the world's arena. I cannot say that their wrestling is always done in the way that seems best to my old eyes, but I admire the Divine order that evidently lays upon each generation its own work, to be done in its own way; and I am convinced that, whether it may seem to us for good or for ill, the generation that is passing must give place to the one that is coming, and must keep hands off from interfering. Advice we who are older may give, and the fruits of our experience, but we must be perfectly content to have our advice rejected by the younger generation, and our experience ignored. Were we willing for this, I am convinced the young would much more often be glad to profit by what is called the "wisdom of the old"; but, as it is, they are afraid to ask advice because they know they will be expected to follow it, whether it commends itself to them or not, and because they fear the old will feel hurt if they do not. Perfect freedom in asking advice can only exist along with perfect freedom not to follow that advice.

I am not of course referring to children, but to the adults of two generations, and I believe, as a general thing, the older generation, when it insists on its advice being taken, puts itself into the unenviable position of being very much in the way of the world's progress. It is found necessary in all lines of business nowadays to employ younger and younger workers, because the older workers are inclined to get into ruts, and are unwilling to be urged out of them. In this connection it is very striking to notice in the history of the Israelites how at the age of fifty they were, by the Divine order, retired from public service, whether in the Tabernacle or in the Army. "And from the age of fifty years they shall cease waiting upon the service thereof, and shall serve no more." It is manifest therefore that, if *they* were retired at fifty, one who is seventy, is at perfect liberty to stand aside from the world's work, and to enjoy that delicious sense of release from responsibility which is the happy privilege of old age.

We read a great deal about the old educating the young. We need just as much that the young should educate the old. I hear that there is a University in Brussels that carries out this idea. It is called the New University, and it is indeed new, for not only do the Professors hold classes for the pupils, but the pupils hold classes for the Professors; and I venture to predict that that University will produce results far beyond those of any other. It is not that I think the wisdom is all shut up in the young, but I am convinced that it is the divine plan that each generation shall have the guidance of its own era, and shall do its work in its own way. And any effort to upset this Divine order, efforts which I am sorry to say we old people are constantly being tempted to make, are sure to produce friction and to hinder progress.

People talk a great deal about the duties the young owe to the old, but I think it is far more important to consider the duties the old owe to the young. I do not of course say that the young owe us old people no duties, but at the age of seventy I have learned to see that the weight of preponderance is enormously on the other side, and that each generation owes to the succeeding one far more duty than the succeeding one owes to them. We brought the younger generation into the world, without consulting them, and we are bound therefore to sacrifice ourselves for their good. This is what the God who created us has done in the sacrifice of Christ, and I do not see that He could have done less. He has poured Himself out without stint for His children, and we must do the same for ours.

Having discovered the unselfishness of God, as every one who has lived to be seventy ought to have done, our attitude towards all around us, should be, up to our measure, one of a similar unselfishness. And surely this is what our Lord wants to teach us when He urges us to love our enemies, and to bless them that curse us, and do good to them that hate us; in order, He says, that we may be the children of our Father which is in Heaven, who Himself does these things. And He ends His words with the exhortation, "Be ye therefore perfect, even as your Father which is in Heaven is perfect." Our perfection therefore is to be the perfection of unselfish love; and, the older we are, the more fully we ought to know this and act on it.

Everything is safe when an unselfish love is guiding and controlling, and therefore my old heart is at rest, and I can lay down my arms with a happy confidence that, since God is in His Heaven, all must necessarily be right with His world, let the "seemings" be what they may. And I can peacefully wait to understand what seems mysterious now, until the glorious day of revelations, to which every hour brings me nearer.

It is to me a most comforting discovery, to have found out that God can manage His own universe Himself, and that He can do it even without my help. I never look at the sun, or the moon, or the stars, without a satisfying recognition of the fact that they are all the "work of His fingers," and that the management of them is His business and not mine, and that therefore I can afford to die and leave them, and all things else, to His care, without a fear that the universe will be dislocated by my going. God is the Housekeeper of His own creation, and just as I should think it folly to worry myself over the housekeeping of my neighbors in Grosvenor Road, so does it seem to me even a greater folly to worry myself over the house-keeping of God. Therefore with an easy mind I can look forward to death, and the prospect of leaving this life and of entering into the larger and grander life beyond, is pure bliss to me. It is like having a new country, full of unknown marvels, to explore; and the knowledge that no one and nothing can hinder my going there, is a secret spring of joy in the bottom of my heart continually. Often and often, when some pleasant earthly plan is spoiled, I say to myself triumphantly, "Ah well, there is one thing about which I can never be disappointed, and that is dying. No one, not even an enemy, can deprive me of that!" Whenever I see a funeral I laugh inwardly at the fresh realization of the fact that such a happy fate lies before every one of us; and I hardly dare trust myself to try writing letters of condolence about the death of any one, for they are almost sure to turn into letters of congratulation at the happy escape of another prisoner from this earthly prison house.

In the different associations to which I belong my comrades never dare ask me to conduct a memorial service for our departed members, for fear I shall be tempted to give thanks for their release. Even for the going home of those I love, I can always rejoice, for it seems to me nothing but selfishness to let my loss outweigh their glorious gain.

I love Walt Whitman's matchless death song, and always want to send it to every dying friend:

> "Joy, shipmate, joy.
> (Pleased to the soul at death, I cry.)
> Our life is closed, our life begins;
> The long, long anchorage we leave,
> The ship is clear at last, she leaps,
> She swiftly courses from the shore!
> Joy, shipmate, joy!"

This passing life with all its affairs, once apparently so important, fades into insignificance in the face of the surpassing life beyond, and I am glad to be so nearly through with it. Its interest has gone for me; and I, who used to be so eager to see every new place, and to taste every new experience, care for them no longer. I have a most satisfactory feeling of being done with this earth. All places look alike to me, and all experiences seem tame in comparison with that which awaits me on the other side.

As to what that is, I can only have vague ideas. I am like the butterfly, just preparing to slip out of its old cocoon, panting for the life outside, but with no experience to tell it what sort of a life that outside life will be. Only I believe with all my heart that the Apostle told the truth when he declared that "eye hath not seen, nor ear heard, neither have entered into the heart of man the things which God hath prepared for them that love Him." And what more delicious prospect could the soul have! I remember vividly my perfect delight many years ago in the prospect of exploring the unknown beauties of the Yellowstone Park, and of the Hoodoo Mountains in Wyoming Territory, a delight caused largely by the fact that they were unknown, and that therefore anything and everything seemed possible. But that delight was as nothing compared to my delight now, in looking forward to the things which have not even entered my mind to conceive.

The one thing I do know about it is, that then will be fulfilled the prayer of our Lord, "Father, I will that they also, whom Thou has given me, be with me where I am, that they may behold my glory which Thou hast given me." That glory is not the glory of dazzling light and golden brightness, as some might picture it, but it is the glory of unselfish love, than which there can be no greater. I have had a few faint glimpses of this glory now and here, and it has been enough to ravish my heart. But there I shall see Him as He is, in all the glory of an infinite unselfishness which no heart of man has ever been able to conceive; and I await the moment with joy.

CHRISTIAN HERALD
People Making A Difference

Christian Herald is a family of dedicated, Christ-centered ministries that reaches out to deprived children in need, and to homeless men who are lost in alcoholism and drug addiction. Christian Herald also offers the finest in family and evangelical literature through its book clubs and publishes a popular, dynamic magazine for today's Christians.

Our Ministries

Family Bookshelf and **Christian Bookshelf** provide a wide selection of inspirational reading and Christian literature written by best-selling authors. All books are recommended by an Advisory Board of distinguished writers and editors.

Christian Herald magazine is contemporary, a dynamic publication that addresses the vital concerns of today's Christian. Each monthly issue contains a sharing of true personal stories written by people who have found in Christ the strength to make a difference in the world around them.

Christian Herald Children. The door of God's grace opens wide to give impoverished youngsters a breath of fresh air, away from the evils of the streets. Every summer, hundreds of youngsters are welcomed at the Christian Herald Mont Lawn Camp located in the Poconos at Bushkill, Pennsylvania. Year-round assistance is also provided, including teen programs, tutoring in reading and writing, family counseling, career guidance and college scholarship programs.

The Bowery Mission. Located in New York City, the Bowery Mission offers hope and Gospel strength to the downtrodden and homeless. Here, the men of Skid Row are fed, clothed, ministered to. Many voluntarily enter a 6-month discipleship program of spiritual guidance, nutrition therapy and Bible study.

Our Father's House. Located in rural Pennsylvania, Our Father's House is a discipleship and job training center. Alcoholics and drug addicts are given an opportunity to recover, away from the temptations of city streets.

Christian Herald ministries, founded in 1878, are supported by the voluntary contributions of individuals and by legacies and bequests. Contributions are tax deductible. Checks should be made out to Christian Herald Children, The Bowery Mission, or to Christian Herald Association.

Administrative Office: 40 Overlook Drive, Chappaqua, New York 10514
Telephone: (914) 769-9000

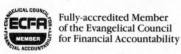 Fully-accredited Member
of the Evangelical Council
for Financial Accountability